Minimum Fee for

or

Basic Conducting Techniques

third edition

Basic Conducting Techniques

JOSEPH A. LABUTA

Wayne State University

Prentice Hall, Englewood Cliffs, New Jersey 07632

Library of Congress Cataloging-in-Publication Data

LABUTA, JOSEPH A.
    Basic conducting techniques / Joseph A. Labuta.—3rd ed.
        p.   cm.
    Includes music.
    Includes bibliographical references and index.
    ISBN 0-13-307257-6
    1. Conducting.   I. Title.
MT85.L24   1995
781.45—dc20   94-26505
                                                      CIP
                                                      MN

Acquisitions editor: *Norwell F. Therien*
Editorial/production supervision
    and interior design: *Carole R. Crouse*
Copy editor: *Carole R. Crouse*
Cover designer: *Wendy Alling Judy*
Buyer: *Bob Anderson*

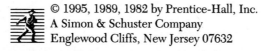 © 1995, 1989, 1982 by Prentice-Hall, Inc.
A Simon & Schuster Company
Englewood Cliffs, New Jersey 07632

Printed in the United States of America
10 9 8 7 6 5 4 3 2 1

ISBN 0-13-307257-6

PRENTICE-HALL INTERNATIONAL (UK) LIMITED, *London*
PRENTICE-HALL OF AUSTRALIA PTY. LIMITED, *Sydney*
PRENTICE-HALL CANADA INC., *Toronto*
PRENTICE-HALL HISPANOAMERICANA, S.A., *Mexico*
PRENTICE-HALL OF INDIA PRIVATE LIMITED, *New Delhi*
PRENTICE-HALL OF JAPAN, INC., *Tokyo*
SIMON & SCHUSTER ASIA PTE. LTD., *Singapore*
EDITORA PRENTICE-HALL DO BRASIL, LTDA., *Rio de Janeiro*

Mux

Contents

Preface, ix

Introduction, 1

PART I   Conducting Technique   5

learning module
ONE

The Baton, Preparation, Downbeat, and Release, 5

learning module
TWO

Beat Patterns and Preparations in Tempo, Dynamic, and Basic Style, 13

learning module
THREE

Preparations and Releases for All Counts, 19

learning module
FOUR

Fractional Beat Preparations, 25

learning module
FIVE

Divided Meters, 28

learning module
SIX   *Conducting Musical Styles, 31*

learning module
SEVEN   *The Fermata, 35*

learning module
EIGHT   *The Cue, 43*

learning module
NINE   *The Left Hand, 45*

learning module
TEN   *Asymmetrical and Changing Meters, 52*

learning module
ELEVEN   *Tempo Changes and Accompanying, 57*

PART II   Score Preparation
and Rehearsal Technique   63

learning module
TWELVE   *Analysis and Score Preparation, 63*

learning module
THIRTEEN   *The Instrumental Rehearsal, 68*

learning module
FOURTEEN   *The Choral Rehearsal, 77*

PART III   Musical Excerpts   83

Learning Module One, 83
Learning Module Two, 85
Learning Module Three, 100
Learning Module Four, 112
Learning Module Five, 119
Learning Module Six, 132
Learning Module Seven, 146

Learning Module Eight, 168

Learning Module Nine, 180

Learning Module Ten, 204

Learning Module Eleven, 229

Learning Module Twelve, 255

appendix A　　*Competencies for the Beginning Conducting Class, 305*

appendix B　　*Student Evaluation, 307*

appendix C　　*Chart of Transpositions and Clefs, 310*

appendix D　　*Full Score Instrumentation and Foreign Equivalents, 311*

appendix E　　*Counting Drills for Uneven Meters, 312*

appendix F　　*Musical Style Chart, 314*

Selected References, 317

Index of Musical Excerpts, 319

Preface

The purpose of the third edition remains the same as that of the previous two: to provide practical procedures and materials for the beginning conducting class. It features a broad repertory of musical excerpts and scores from the standard literature, more varied selections for class use than any other available source. It retains the same basic format, since students and instructors have responded favorably to the conductor-competency approach to student learning. This student-oriented workbook includes clearly stated outcomes and performance tests for student guidance, actual conducting activities for student learning, and varied musical examples for the student to study, practice, conduct, and rehearse. The learner can work with an ensemble of class members, since most excerpts are reduced to a four-part score format. This allows every learner to practice conducting skills and rehearsal techniques at each class meeting. Thus, the book fulfills several basic needs for teaching conducting in the classroom setting. Using this text, the student can study the learning modules and scores, and conduct a live performing group using valid repertory selected to facilitate learning by emphasizing conducting and rehearsal problems.

The third edition facilitates even broader usage with the addition of choral music excerpts, choral scores, and choral rehearsal techniques. It makes the workbook more appropriate for mixed classes of choral and instrumental music majors. Just as the text has proven valuable as a tool to introduce the prospective choral director to instrumental conducting, the choral techniques can help prepare instrumental music majors to conduct choral groups. Versatility can be a great advantage when pursuing music-teaching positions. The instrumental rehearsal technique section is expanded further, and a band score is now included for study, rehearsal, and conducting.

This workbook also provides an excellent review of conducting technique for graduate students and practicing conductors.

Joseph A. Labuta

Basic Conducting Techniques

Introduction

Whether you are a student, an instructor, or a practicing conductor, you can bene-fit most from this workbook by becoming familiar with its unique features and var-ied potentials for use. These introductory sections enumerate the book's salient points, discuss the notion of competency-based education, give students sugges-tions for using the learning modules and excerpts, and recommend instructional approaches to the workbook material.

FEATURES OF THIS WORKBOOK

This book's first innovative feature is the repertory it provides for the conducting class. Part III consists of carefully selected examples from the musical literature that illustrate the conducting problems students must solve to develop conducting skills. Since scheduled performance ensembles are usually unobtainable for class use, at least on a regular basis, students must of necessity conduct other class members if they are to gain practical experience with a live performing group. They need appropriate and valid examples from the standard repertory that they can use in a classroom situation. The selected excerpts are reduced to four parts to accommodate classes with limited instrumentation. Most excerpts can be played by a quartet from the same family of instruments, by a heterogeneous quartet, by the entire class, or by a piano with or without additional instruments. The student must solve problems of balance in such varied situations, perhaps designating the instrumentation desired. A few excerpts make use of more than four parts to approximate original sonorities, but choral excerpts are limited to four-part SATB format. If a band, an orchestra, or a chorus is available, or if the composition of the class is adequate, the student should also study and conduct the complete full scores represented by the excerpts.

A second unique feature of this workbook is the use of student competencies in the form of clearly stated course objectives. "Competence" refers to the ability to do something. The conducting competencies define precisely what a beginning conductor must demonstrate to complete the course. Appendix A consists of a complete listing of the competencies used in this book. They were derived by an analysis of the essential skills a beginning conductor should develop to lead and rehearse a performing group. Each competency is at once the learning outcome the student must demonstrate and the conducting problem he or she must solve. The stated competencies guide student learning and provide a sound basis for instruction and evaluation.

A third important feature is the built-in provision for continuing student evaluation. The workbook supplies tests and evaluative criteria including rating scales, checklists, and analytical guides. Each section contains a self-check mastery test to inform students of progress. The videocassette recorder is an important tool for this evaluation and for instruction. Each mastery test has a VCR checklist for student self-evaluation. However, if no VCR is available, faculty or peers can administer and evaluate the tests. The final examination is in the form of a "Conducting Competence Rating Scale," designed to evaluate all the stated competencies. The rating scale, located in Appendix B, should be used frequently toward the end of the course sequence.

A fourth feature is the organization of the workbook for student learning. The text is in "modular" format. Each module contains learning objectives, instruction, practice activities, and testing procedures. Students can work through the book systematically, module by module; yet, the instructor has unrestricted flexibility in its use. Since essential prerequisite knowledge and skills are acquired in the first three modules, instructor and student can decide on any sequence of the later modules to accommodate individual needs. For example, the instructor may utilize a cyclic approach, returning students to a module for remedial work, or for mastering needed competencies.

The fifth distinctive feature of this workbook relates to the problem-solving nature of conducting. Regardless of the sequence of modules a student may follow, learning is best initiated and facilitated by grappling with the conducting problems encountered in the music to be performed. Therefore, the musical score is the basic element of this workbook. The score presents the problems the conductor must solve to become competent. This problem-centered approach helps avoid the atomization and mechanization of learning that is always a potential danger with the modular format. The complex skills acquired by a master conductor are certainly more than the sum of their parts. The music in this workbook represents the synthesis or "gestalt" within which the problems are found, whereas the learning module (where each part can be examined, practiced, and, if necessary, drilled out of context) provides the analysis phase of the process.

Conducting problems are essentially of two types: those of conception and those of execution.

Problems of Conception

Conception refers to the conductor's inner hearing of the correct performance. Students gain it through score study. This inner hearing of the score is the only sound basis for interpreting music and for developing conducting/rehearsal technique. According to Bruno Walter, a most important aim of studying the score is the gradual acquisition of a distinct, inner "sound image" or "sound ideal"; this will establish itself in the ear of the conductor as a criterion that exerts a guiding and controlling influence over his or her practical music making.* Thus, the physical action patterns that the student is attempting to learn are controlled and guided by the desired musical result. This workbook helps the instructor to evaluate the stu-

---

*Bruno Walter, *Of Music and Music-Making*, trans. Paul Hamburger (New York: W. W. Norton & Company, Inc., 1961), p. 85.

dent's knowledge of the score by providing checklists and other observational techniques, such as having the student sing through each part, arpeggiate the harmony, identify errors, write score analyses, play the score on the piano, and give correct transpositions.

Problems of Execution

The student must develop readable conducting gestures that represent appropriate attacks and releases, tempo, meter, style, dynamics, balance, cuing, accentuation, phrasing, and interpretation. He or she must be able to rehearse by detecting and correcting errors of performance. Learners acquire conducting and rehearsal competencies most efficiently by solving the problems contained in the music, not by practicing techniques in isolation. Thus, the excerpts in this book were chosen to emphasize particular technical or interpretive problems, and the preparation, rehearsal, and performance of these scores represent the principal barriers to be overcome for learning. Since the aural concept guides development, techniques are never ends in themselves but means to achieve expressive performance. Technical development is not separated from actual music, and therefore students can perceive the relationship between manual technique and the desired musical outcome. Instructor and student can evaluate technical learning by using the check sheets and rating scales provided in the workbook.

THE COMPETENCY-BASED APPROACH

"Competency" refers to the capacity to perform specified tasks up to a standard. Competency-based programs begin with the specification or definition of what constitutes competence in a given field or profession. The student must then demonstrate the ability to do something with the subject-matter content, at the level described in a competency statement.

A competency curriculum consists of three principal components: the explicit statement of the competencies that students must demonstrate, the specification of criteria for assessing students' mastery of competencies, and the provision of alternative learning activities presented in modules to facilitate student attainment and demonstration of the competencies. In the competency approach, students accept responsibility for learning, that is, for achieving the competencies at a criterion level. They compile evidence that they have attained competence through demonstrations, videotapes, checklists, rating scales, portfolios, and certification by the faculty.

TO THE STUDENT

This workbook is designed primarily for you, the student. It consists of learning modules with materials for you to study, and musical excerpts from the standard literature for you to conduct. A learning module is a type of individualized curriculum package that is intended to help you acquire and demonstrate specified conducting competencies. Each module includes five essential parts: an overview, competency statements, instruction, conducting activities, and a mastery test.

The "Overview" summarizes the conducting problems to be solved in the module and describes the rationale or purpose for attaining the competencies.

The "Competencies" were derived by an analysis of the important skills the beginning conductor must develop to lead a musical group. These statements tell you at the outset of each module what knowledge and technique you should be able to demonstrate by the end of it. The attainment of that knowledge and technique enables you to beat through all types of conducting problems effectively and to rehearse musical groups efficiently.

The "Instruction" sections present information, explanations, illustrations, and directions for achieving the competencies.

The various "Conducting Activities" are designed to facilitate learning and offer opportunities to practice the skills specified in the competencies. The majority of the activities give you actual conducting experience in class by using the excerpts in Part III of the workbook. Develop your rehearsal technique by making *at least* one correction *every* time you conduct during the early modules. Later, rehearse consistently and thoroughly.

The "Self-Check Mastery Test" will allow you to gauge your progress by evaluating your videotaped performances, and to demonstrate attainment of the module objectives. By using the checklist for self-criticism, you take responsibility for your own learning and define your own conducting problems and technical difficulties. Your identified weaknesses then become your daily course objectives.

Follow this recommended approach to master each module:

1. Scan the module; note particularly the mastery test. Can you pass it? What do you need to learn?

2. Familiarize yourself with the objectives (competency statements) to guide your learning.

3. Study information, illustrations, and instructions. Study and analyze appropriate excerpts to gain aural conception. Observe your instructor's demonstrations, and listen carefully to his or her explanations. If necessary, write in transpositions for the parts you will play in class.

4. Seek opportunities to practice the activities in and out of class until you have reached the required skill level.

5. Use videotaping for self-evaluation and improvement.

6. Demonstrate conducting competence by passing the mastery test.

TO THE INSTRUCTOR

This competency-based text provides a systematic presentation of basic conducting skills in modular format. Yet, you can take several approaches to the material.

You may direct students to begin with Part I and progress through the modules in the order presented. The modules are arranged in a logical learning sequence. Working through the modules in succession is a thorough pedagogical approach suited to the learning styles of most students.

You may, however, prefer to start with the musical excerpts in Part III and then demonstrate techniques, explain problems, evaluate performance, and generally teach in any way you wish. Since the modules are directed to the student, not the instructor, they can be self-teaching and self-paced if students use them for independent study. In this sense, the modules support class instruction.

A third approach is to begin study with the analysis and score preparation module in Part II, in which students thoroughly analyze and prepare music before they attempt to conduct it.

Regardless of the instructional approach you may choose, there should always be an interplay among the modules in Part I, the modules in Part II, and the musical excerpts in Part III. Students can gain most from the workbook through this interactive process.

learning module **ONE**

The Baton, Preparation, Downbeat, and Release

OVERVIEW

This module requires you to conduct a live musical ensemble, even if you have no previous conducting experience. To make certain you succeed at this task, you must concentrate on beat preparation. The sharply defined and well-executed preparatory beat is the basic gesture you must develop to establish competent musical leadership from the podium. All effective conducting is preparatory in function, in that musicians can only respond or react *to* a gesture; they cannot react simultaneously with an unprepared gesture. To forget this basic fact invites conducting failure. This module, based on the preeminence of preparation, provides a solid foundation for all that is to come.

Your first conducting problem, then, is to secure a precise, unified attack from the group, followed by an equally precise release. In this module, you will learn to hold a baton, to assume the preparatory position, to execute the preparatory beat and downbeat with rebound, and to give a release. You can make the best use of the analysis of conducting motions provided in the modules when your aural conception ("inner hearing") of desired musical results guides and controls your physical action patterns.

HOLDING THE BATON

▶ **COMPETENCY 1**
Demonstrate appropriate baton grip

The baton is the symbol of leadership authority for the conductor. It is also a conductor's technical, if not musical, instrument. By extending the forearm, a baton gives clarity to the beat and the conducting pattern. By providing better visibility for performers, it facilitates precision in ensemble performance. Although some authorities argue that the baton limits expressiveness, the skilled conductor can use it to infuse beat patterns with stylistic qualities while using the left hand to

ILLUSTRATION 1-1
Holding the Baton

indicate phrasing and expression (see Modules Six and Nine). Every conducting student should use a baton and hold it in the right hand. Students may, of course, defer to custom and conduct the choral repertory without a baton. However, it seems more difficult to begin using a baton after learning to conduct without one than to take the opposite approach.

Instruction

To hold the baton most effectively, rest the ball end against the palm of the hand with the shaft held securely, yet flexibly, between the tip of the thumb and the side of the index finger at the first joint. The thumb should curve slightly, and the remaining fingers also curve naturally around the stick without touching it. (See Illustration 1-1.) This provides for wrist flexibility quite similar to that found in holding and playing a drumstick, with the palm of the hand facing downward. Although you should feel that the baton extends straight out from the arm, it will point slightly to the left when the ball is centered properly in the palm.

Conducting Activities

1. Obtain a ball-end baton about fourteen inches in length. Practice holding the baton as just described.
2. Use a mirror to check holding position and baton angle.
3. Tap the tip of the baton on a chest-high object to practice wrist flexibility.

ILLUSTRATION 1-2
The Preparatory Position for Starting Music
on the Count of One in All Meters

THE PREPARATORY POSITION

▶ ***COMPETENCY 2.1***

Demonstrate the preparatory position for starting on the count of one in all meters

Conductors must use the preparatory position as a signal for the group to get ready to start playing. It secures initial attention and gives musicians time to raise their instruments to playing position. Use a podium for optimal visibility. Make certain the players' stands are adjusted to the proper height and positioned directly between you and them. When the stands are positioned properly, the players can see you easily with both direct and peripheral vision. Have singers hold their music up about eye level in their left hand so that they can watch you as they read and use their right hand to turn pages. Adjust the conductor's stand to an almost flat position at waist height so it does not hide your beats or patterns.

Instruction

Ascend the podium in a confident, authoritative manner. Stand erect; balanced, with feet slightly separated; and poised, yet relaxed, not tense. Raise your arms upward and outward with elbows slightly away from your body. (See Illustration 1-2.) This preparatory position should be easily visible, and commanding and positive in appearance. It is the signal for the group to get ready. Allow several seconds to make a quick visual check to make certain all instruments are in playing position and all musicians are looking at you. Maintain visual contact through the downbeat. Musicians and conductor should memorize the first few measures to assure a precise attack. Never talk with your hands in preparatory position and never wait too long before beginning. This causes musicians' attention to wander and instruments to lower from ready position.

Conducting Activities

1. Ascend a podium and practice the preparatory position. Repeat this important exercise several times to become secure and confident with the stance.
2. Use a mirror to check the position of body, arms, hands, and baton.

PREPARATORY BEAT

▶ ***COMPETENCY 3.1****

Demonstrate the preparatory beat for the count of one, i.e., for the downbeat in all meters

All effective conducting involves preparation. Preparatory or anticipatory gestures give an inevitability to conducting that results in ensemble precision. Musicians cannot respond at the instant of a single gesture; they respond to a prepared gesture. Thus, effective conducting always signals *"ready—go,"* never just "go."

The preparatory beat is one extra beat (sometimes one-half beat) that precedes the first beat of music. It is a breathing beat. You should always inhale when you expect the musicians to breathe. Their response seems almost instinctive. Even strings and percussion will breathe with you to achieve greater precision and expression. A preparatory gesture, then, must precede every initial entrance and every resumption of the musical line.

Instruction

To prepare the count of one in any meter, assume the preparatory position, flick a point of beat with your wrist, and breathe in as you swing up on the offbeat. Do not hesitate at the top but move straight down to the count of one (see Figure 1-1). As a rule, conduct in front of your body, not to one side, so that the downbeat is centered. Always maintain eye contact through the performance of the downbeat.

FIGURE 1-1
The Preparatory Beat for One

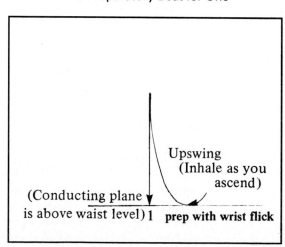

*You will note that the competencies as they come up in the text are *not* in their correct numbered sequence. See Appendix A for the complete list of competencies.

Conducting Activities

1. Practice the preparatory beat for the count of one. Think "prep—one" in various tempos. Do not hesitate at the top; to do so will disrupt the inevitable fall of the gesture to its termination at the count of one.

2. The best way to illustrate "beat inevitability" is to use the "key toss." Take a set of keys or some other object, toss it about two feet in the air, and catch it. Have musicians perform a chord at the point of contact. A precise attack results because the performers know exactly when the keys will hit. Good conductors develop this type of inevitability in the arcs of their beats and patterns by beating on a consistent level and using a follow-through as natural as a bouncing ball.

WRIST ACTION

▶ **COMPETENCY 4**
Demonstrate proper wrist action to define the exact point of beat

The consummation of the preparatory gesture as it arrives through the downstroke is the count of one. This point is defined precisely by a small snap of the wrist. This subtle but vital wrist action is variously called the rebound, flick, click, bounce, recoil, or *ictus*. The beat, as a point in time, must be exactly identified by the tip of the baton through flexible and suitable wrist action. If you do not use a baton, place the point of beat in the index finger.

Instruction

Give the preparatory gesture and rebound off the plane of beating at the count of one, using a flexible wrist action (see Figure 1-2). Do not excessively flop or turn your wrist. You should keep your palm facing downward and rebound no more than one-fourth the distance of the downbeat.

FIGURE 1-2
The Rebound on One

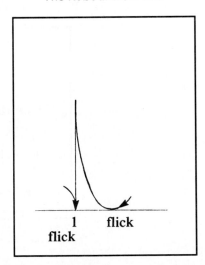

1   flick
flick

Conducting Activities

1. Practice the preparation for one with a rebound on the count of one. Think "prep—tap" in various tempos, rebounding off the plane of beating.

2. If you have trouble with wrist flexibility, think of flicking something off the end of the baton, or think of hitting an imaginary plane. You can actually tap a chest-high bookcase or music stand to get the feel of correct wrist action for the rebound.

THE RELEASE

▶   ***COMPETENCY 5.1***
Demonstrate the basic release gesture

The release gesture is a concise cutoff, a precise signal to cease playing. To secure precision, a preparatory gesture, usually a circular motion, must precede it. Just as a "ready—go" must be given at the beginning of a composition, so a "ready—stop" must be indicated at the end.

Instruction

Execute the release gesture with a small circular motion; the cutoff comes at the end of the preparatory arc with a flick of the wrist. Give the circular motion in a clockwise or a counterclockwise direction, depending on the starting position required for any succeeding preparatory beat (see Figure 1-3). Be careful not to overemphasize the cutoff for the sake of clarity. The players may respond with a crescendo or a sforzando.

  To conduct the release after the count of one, start with the preparatory beat, follow through with a downbeat to the count of one, and execute a cutoff in tempo. By releasing to the right, you will logically end up in position to repeat the preparation (see Figure 1-4).

FIGURE 1-3
Circular Preparation and Cutoff Flick

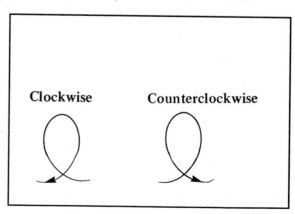

Clockwise   Counterclockwise

FIGURE 1-4
Preparing One and Releasing

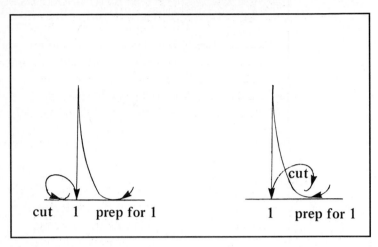

Conducting Activities

1. Practice the preparatory beat for the count of one, followed by a release gesture as illustrated in Figure 1-4. Think "prep—one—cut," keeping the beat steady and pausing briefly between each repetition.
2. Use different metronome settings as you work on this technique.
3. Conduct the class or some colleagues in a series of one-count notes and releases. Work for clear, effective gestures in your conducting and precise attacks from the performers.

SELF-CHECK MASTERY TEST

1. Conduct excerpts 1-1 through 1-5 in Part III, as requested by the instructor, in class with a videocassette recorder. Conduct each excerpt using a preparatory beat, a downbeat, and a release gesture. Think "prep—one—cut" in tempo, with a pause between each note. Repeat in any tempo given by the instructor.
2. Rate your VCR performances by using the following checklists.* If a VCR is unavailable, have colleagues or your instructor complete the form.

*By using pencils or pens of different colors, you should be able to use this checklist a number of times.

BATON-HOLDING POSITION

Yes   No

___ ___   Baton held between thumb and index finger
___ ___   Grip firm, but flexible, not tense
___ ___   Fingers curved naturally
___ ___   Palm facing downward
___ ___   Baton extends almost straight from arm

PREPARATORY POSITION

Yes   No

___ ___   Posture erect, poised, relaxed
___ ___   Stance commanding, positive
___ ___   Arms raised, easily visible
___ ___   Baton in position for preparatory beat to follow
___ ___   Visual check made to ensure readiness of group
___ ___   Sufficient time allowed for group to get instruments in position, set embouchures, and generally get ready to perform
___ ___   Never talks with hands in preparatory position or otherwise takes too much time

PREPARATORY BEAT, DOWNBEAT, AND REBOUND

Yes   No

___ ___   Preparatory beat initiated on plane with wrist flick
___ ___   Breathes in with upswing of baton
___ ___   Prep executed without hesitation
___ ___   Downbeat straight down in front of body
___ ___   Point of beat defined with rebound
___ ___   Wrist action flexible; palm facing down
___ ___   Rebound proper height (about 1/4 downbeat)
___ ___   Visual contact maintained through downbeat
___ ___   Group attack precise

THE RELEASE

Yes   No

___ ___   Properly prepared with small circular motion
___ ___   Cutoff indicated by wrist flick
___ ___   Clear, accurate, but not overconducted

Beat Patterns and Preparations in Tempo, Dynamic, and Basic Style

OVERVIEW

This module is designed primarily to facilitate your learning the standard conducting patterns for the meters of one, two, three, and four. You will conduct music in these meters maintaining a steady and appropriate tempo. The module also instructs you to conduct preparatory beats that indicate tempo, dynamic level, and style for entrances on the count of one.

STANDARD CONDUCTING PATTERNS

▶ **COMPETENCY 6**
Demonstrate the standard beat patterns, maintaining a steady tempo

The standard conducting patterns evolved with metric music. Ideally, these hand motions serve to portray visually the sounding structure of the meter, placing strong and weak metric accents appropriately in the pattern. For example, the first beat gesture is longer and stronger and in all cases must move straight down.

Conducting patterns have other advantages. Musicians know them and can follow them more easily than random gestures. The consistent downbeat is certainly helpful when players are insecure or lost. Yet beat patterns do have certain limitations, and it is possible for a conductor to become little more than a time-beater. Interpretation suffers when beat patterns are overemphasized, and phrasing and expression are slighted. The solution to the problem is to infuse beat patterns with expressive qualities to facilitate phrasing, style, and expression (see Modules Six and Nine).

FIGURE 2-1
Basic Rules of Pattern Construction

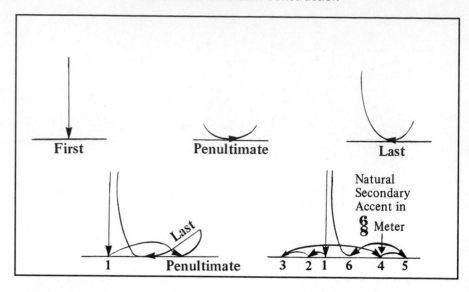

Instruction

The standard conducting patterns present a visual image of meter structure to musicians, and you must use them if you are to gain clarity and consistency. A few general principles govern all beat patterns, as Figure 2-1 illustrates.

1. The first and strongest beat is down.
2. The penultimate (second to last) beat moves to the right.
3. The last beat swings in to the left, then up.
4. All beats hit an imaginary, horizontal surface located above waist level.
5. Additional beats are placed laterally on the plane of beating, with the secondary accents given the most emphasis by longer gestures.

FIGURE 2-2
Incorrect Conducting Diagrams

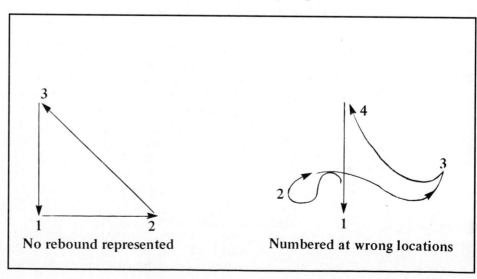

FIGURE 2-3
The "V" Shaped and "U" Shaped Conducting Motions

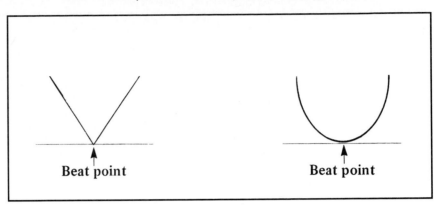

Beat point   Beat point

Many traditional conducting diagrams are misleading because either they do not depict the rebound from the point of beat or they place the number representing the point of beat at the wrong location, usually at the end of the rebound (see Figure 2-2).

The modules provide diagrams with arrows to indicate the exact points of beat, and show two basic pattern shapes or motions: the "V" shape and the "U" shape (see Figure 2-3). Note that the point of beat is always at the bottom of these motions on the plane of beating. Thus, every beat is a type of downward motion followed by a rebound.

The tip of the baton taps the imaginary plane with wrist action to define the exact point of beat. If your wrist is stiff and tense, the focal point of the beat will be centered incorrectly and unclearly in your hand or forearm. Although you must use forearm movement from the elbow to enlarge wrist motion and trace patterns, do not allow the elbow itself to move excessively. Conduct in front of your body, not to one side, maintaining a steady, even tempo.

In Figure 2-4 (p. 16), each pattern is drawn to represent the two basic styles of legato and staccato. If the beats in a pattern are connected by smooth, flowing gestures, they express legato style. If the gestures are choppy and disconnected, they express staccato style.

Conducting Activities

1. Practice all conducting patterns until they become automatic. Do this often, at any odd times you can find, to develop complete technical mastery. For two, think "down-rebound, in-rebound." For three, think "down-rebound, right-rebound, in-rebound." For four, think "down-rebound, left-rebound, right-rebound, in-rebound," etc.

2. Check the clarity and style of your patterns in the mirror.

3. Practice tapping the tip of the baton on a music stand or cabinet that is above waist level to get the feeling for proper, flexible wrist action in a pattern on a plane of beating. Move directly into beats; never float down and poke at them with the hand and forearm.

4. If you have difficulty feeling and maintaining a steady pulse in your baton motions, practice with a metronome at various tempo settings, e.g., MM. 60, 96, 120, 132, and 160. Practice simultaneously walking and conducting to put the physical feel for the beat into the baton.

FIGURE 2-4
Basic Conducting Patterns

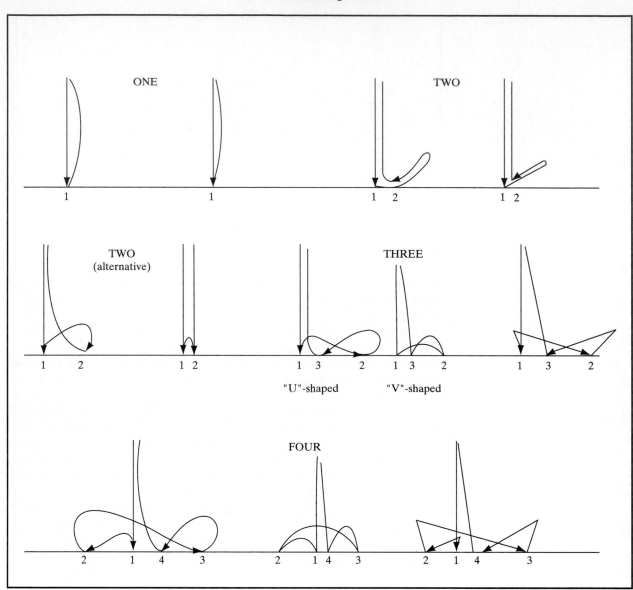

THE PREPARATORY BEAT

▶ **COMPETENCY 3.2**
Demonstrate the preparatory beat for the count of one that indicates appropriate tempo, dynamic level, and style of the music being performed

A competent conductor is able to start a group with precision by using a single count of preparation. The one-count preparation must also convey the exact tempo, dynamic level, and style of the music to follow. The conducting gesture consists of more than arm movement, however. It includes inhalation, physiognomy (facial expression), and chin motion (subtle head nod) on the beginning upbeat, and it should radiate tempo and expression. This section is designed to help you develop the complete preparatory gesture for the count of one.

FIGURE 2-5
Preparation Styles

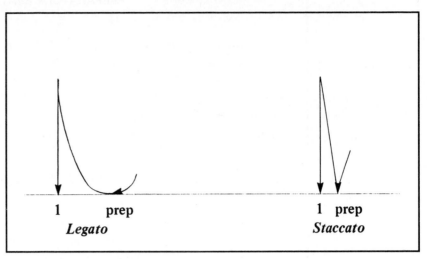

Instruction

To assure exact tempo of preparatory beats and the beats that follow, feel inwardly the pulse of the music; think it and count it to yourself. If you do this, your whole body will radiate the tempo, and your preparatory-beat gesture, reinforced by inhalation and head nod, will be convincing as well as exacting. Dynamically, a forceful, aggressive preparation results in a *forte* attack. A smaller, less aggressive preparation achieves a softer dynamic response. Stylistically, a jerky, choppy preparation indicates staccato; a smooth, flowing one, legato; and a heavy forceful one, marcato (see Figure 2-5 and Module Six). In general, do not count off orally or visually to begin performing, unless reestablishing rhythmic flow within a composition in a rehearsal setting.

Conducting Activities

1. Practice preparatory beats in various tempos, dynamic levels, styles, and meters. Check gestures, breathing, and physiognomy in the mirror.
2. Prepare and conduct excerpts 2-1 through 2-18 in Part III.

SELF-CHECK MASTERY TEST

1. Conduct excerpts 2-1 through 2-18, as requested by the instructor, in class with the videocassette recorder.
2. Use the single preparatory beat that indicates tempo, dynamic, and style of the music you are requested to conduct.
3. Rate your VCR performance by using the following checklists.

PREPARATORY BEATS

Yes	No	
____	____	Preparatory beats executed in appropriate tempo
____	____	Dynamic level indicated
____	____	Style indicated
____	____	Group attack is precise and reflects desired
____	____	tempo,
____	____	dynamic, and
____	____	style

BEAT PATTERNS AND TEMPO

Yes	No	
____	____	Beats are well defined; ictus is clear
____	____	Musicians respond exactly to beat pulsations
____	____	Beats bounce off plane of beating located above waist level
____	____	Wrist, forearm, and elbow function appropriately
____	____	Beats are even and steady, tempo appropriate and steady
____	____	Beat patterns are clear and well defined
____	____	Pattern is positioned in front of body (not to one side)
____	____	Pattern is proportioned properly (not lopsided; certain beats not overemphasized)
____	____	Size of pattern is appropriate for dynamics
____	____	Character of pattern reflects the style of music

Preparations and Releases for All Counts

OVERVIEW

In this module, you learn to start the group and stop it on any required count of music. The module instructs you to use a modified preparatory position. From this position, you can give a preparatory beat in the appropriate direction to lead into any count of any meter pattern at the point where the music begins. You are further instructed to give releases on any ending beat.

THE MODIFIED PREPARATORY POSITION

▶ **COMPETENCY 2.2**
Demonstrate the preparatory position for starting on counts other than one

Module One described the basic attention position to start on the count of one. (You raise your arms upward and outward in position for the preparatory beat, which begins in and up on the final count of all meters.) However, for entrances on a beat *other* than the count of one, you must adjust the basic preparatory position so that the baton is centered in the appropriate location to initiate the preparatory beat to the left or the right.

Instruction

To start on a beat other than the count of one, place your right hand so that the baton is at the center of your body, or somewhat left of center, at about chest level. (See Illustration 3-1.) Use the center or left-of-center position as needed to conduct the preparatory beats described in the next section of the module.

The way that you move into and maintain the position of attention is critical. Many conducting students do not immediately take the appropriate preparatory position, and subsequently attempt to make adjustments just before giving the

19

ILLUSTRATION 3-1
The Preparatory Position for Starting Music on Counts Other Than One

preparatory beat. This action causes players to make false entrances. Remember that musicians react almost instinctively to any upswing motion as a preparatory gesture. In other words, the effect of the last-minute accommodation is to *prepare the preparatory beat* and elicit early responses from the players. Never swing up before a preparatory beat; always stand motionless and move directly into the actual preparatory gesture.

PREPARATORY BEATS FOR OTHER COUNTS

▶ **COMPETENCY 3.3**
Demonstrate the preparatory beat for counts other than one

Compositions often begin on a beat other than one—for instance, after rests or on pickup notes of one or more counts. A problem may arise for beginning conductors in these cases because the basic last-count preparatory gesture does not fit into the subsequent meter scheme. The solution offered by most authorities is logical although somewhat pedantic: Because a preparatory beat consists of one extra count before the first count of music, you should use the direction of the preceding beat of the conducting pattern as the gesture of preparation.

Instruction

As a general rule, use the preceding beat in the meter pattern as the preparatory beat for an entrance. That is, use three if the pickup is on four; use two if the pickup is on three; and so on. The preparatory motion will usually occur in the

FIGURE 3-1
Preparation for All Last Counts

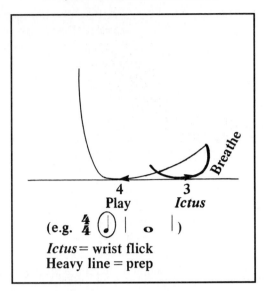

opposite direction from the first sounding beat. However, merely tracing a certain direction with the baton will not necessarily result in a convincing preparation. A prep beat must look like a prep beat, that is, a breathing gesture. Put yourself in the position of the performer and breathe as if you were playing or singing the music.

All preparatory beats are executed by giving an ictus (a flick with the wrist to define the exact point of beat) and then swinging up in tempo while breathing in for preparation. Next you move the baton to the count in the pattern where the music begins.

As the count of one has a consistent preparatory beat direction (see Module One), so the preparation for the last count of all meters is always the same: to the right (see Figure 3-1). Figures 3-2 and 3-3 illustrate other consistent preparatory motions.

FIGURE 3-2
Starting on Beats to the Right of One

FIGURE 3-3
Starting on Beats to the Left of One

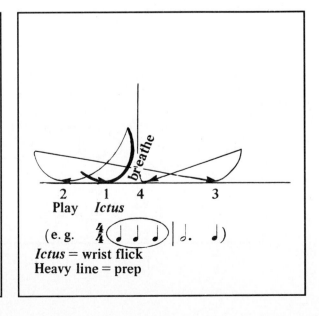

Conducting Activities

1. Practice attention positions and preparatory beats for all counts in all meters. Check your positions and preparations in the mirror for appropriate pattern direction, tempo, dynamics, and style.
2. Prepare excerpts 3-1 through 3-16 in Part III of the workbook.
3. Conduct excerpts in class and use the VCR checklists to evaluate your performance.

RELEASES ON ALL BEATS

▶ **COMPETENCY 5.2**
Demonstrate the release on all counts of all meters

You must be able to execute a clear, precise cutoff wherever one is written in the score. Fortunately, any count of the pattern can be given as a release gesture. It must always be prepared and the exact point of the cutoff defined by an ictus. The release should also match the tempo, dynamic, and style of the music. Except in the case of final notes, the cutoff should be executed so that the baton ends up in position to begin the preparation for the next entrance of music.

Instruction

You can conduct any count of any meter as a release gesture. Use a circular motion with a flick at the bottom of the arc to define the exact point of release. Figure 3-4 provides examples of typical releases on a final eighth note in a meter of four.

You may reinforce the baton release by mirroring the gesture with the left hand or by closing the fingers against the thumb at the cutoff point. Give the release in the tempo, dynamic level, and style of the musical context. Plan the direction of the release gesture in advance, so that you will end the baton motion in position to give the preparatory beat for the next count of music (see Figure 3-5).

FIGURE 3-4
Releases on All Counts of the Four Pattern

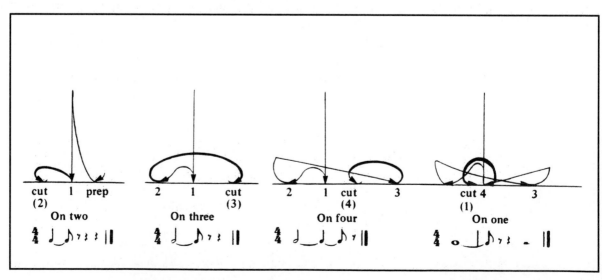

FIGURE 3-5
Release on Four in Position to Prepare One

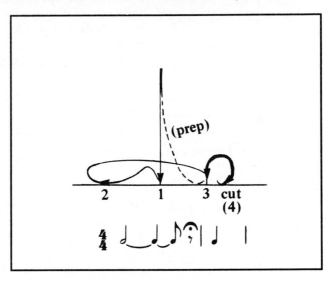

Conducting Activities

1. Practice the release gesture on all counts of all meters. Follow the release with the appropriate preparation for the next count. Think: "one, cut, prep, two, three, four; one, two, cut, prep, three, four; one, two, three, cut, prep, four;" etc., in all meters.
2. Diagram releases if you have trouble visualizing them.
3. Check for clarity, dynamic, and style of your releases by using a mirror.
4. Prepare excerpts 3-1 through 3-16 in Part III.

SELF-CHECK MASTERY TEST ─────────────────────────────────

1. Conduct excerpts 3-1 through 3-16, as requested by the instructor, in class with the videocassette recorder.
2. Use the single preparatory beat that indicates the tempo, dynamic, and style of the music you are requested to conduct.
3. Use an appropriate release gesture for the ending count.
4. Rate your VCR performance by using the following checklists.

PREPARATION

Yes   No

—— —— Preparatory position suitable for prep beat to follow
—— —— Preparatory beat executed in an appropriate direction and
—— ——   in appropriate tempo
—— ——   in appropriate dynamic
—— ——   in appropriate style
—— —— Group response precise

RELEASES

Yes   No

—— —— Releases clear and in tempo
—— —— Releases prepared properly
—— —— Releases in dynamic level of musical context
—— —— Releases in style of musical context
—— —— Releases followed by appropriate and clear preparatory beats

Fractional Beat Preparations

OVERVIEW

This module is designed to facilitate your conducting preparatory beats for music that begins on a fraction of the count. You must learn two basic methods of preparation and be able to select the most appropriate one for the music to be conducted.

FRACTIONAL PICKUP NOTES

▶ **COMPETENCY 3.4**
Demonstrate the preparatory beat that indicates appropriate tempo, dynamic level, and style for fractional pickup notes and between-beat starts

Many musical compositions begin on a fractional unit of the beat. You must decide on the best method of preparation for each composition, and execute it well to elicit a precise, unified response. As a general rule, you should provide either one count or two counts of preparation. Tempo, notation, and musical context provide clues regarding the most effective approach in a given situation.

Instruction

The one-count preparatory   In the *one-count-prep method,* you use the beat count within which the fraction occurs as the preparatory beat. In other words, prepare the first full beat that follows the fraction and subsume the fraction within the preparation. Do not attempt to beat the fraction or otherwise divide the meter. Breathe in quickly with the preparatory upswing, feel the fraction within it, and nod your head to facilitate an exact attack. Follow through with no hesitation at the apex of the preparatory beat.

The two-count preparatory   In the *two-count-prep method,* you beat two counts of preparation. Although the double preparatory establishes the tempo securely and should result in a more unified attack, you must take great care not to bring the musicians in prematurely. The first preparatory must be a neutral or passive beat—one that elicits no response from the players—although it is given in

FIGURE 4-1
Two Methods for Conducting Fractional Pickup Notes

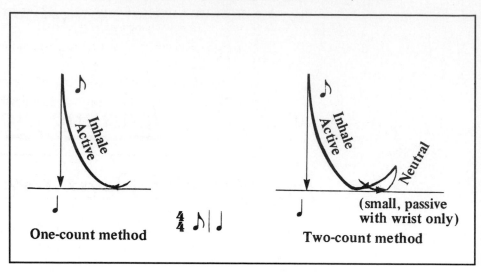

tempo. The second beat must be a "live" preparation, one that demands a response on the fraction. Follow the diagrams in Figure 4-1 to guide your practice.

You should use the one-count method in fairly slow tempos where the beat is easily established or where the fraction occupies less than one-half count. The two-count technique is most appropriate for fast tempos and for instances in which the fraction occupies more than one-half count.

The hybrid approach   A hybrid approach combines the best features of the other two. In this method, you use the left hand to flick the initial preparation—as in the two-beat technique—while holding the baton motionless in preparatory position. Then you employ the right hand to execute the preparation on the beat of the fraction—as in the one-beat technique. If you are careful not to make any extra baton motions, this method secures the tempo and eliminates possible false starts.

Some compositions begin with rests in all parts. For clarity, you should always beat out any initial rests using small, neutral gestures. When the parts are to enter, give a live preparation on the rebound (upswing) of the prior count.

If in doubt about the direction for a preparation for a fraction within a measure (for example, after a rest or a fermata), use a beat-plane wrist flick, followed by an upswing with inhalation. Then move to the next count in the meter pattern. The upward motion always provides a good secure breathing beat.

Conducting Activities

1. Practice fractional-beat entrances in various meters, using each method of preparation. Concentrate on the typical one-half count, fractional pickup note.

2. Prepare and rehearse excerpts 4-1 through 4-12 in Part III of the workbook.

3. Check your positions and beats using the mirror and the VCR checklists.

SELF-CHECK MASTERY TEST ——————————————————

1. Conduct excerpts 4-1 through 4-12, as requested by the instructor, in class with the videocassette recorder.
2. Use the one-count or two-count preparation as requested by the instructor.
3. Demonstrate the "left hand to baton" two-count preparation.
4. Rate your performance by using the following checklists.

ONE-COUNT PREPARATION

Yes   No

_____ _____ Preparatory position suitable for the prep beat to follow
_____ _____ Preparatory beat executed in an appropriate direction, tempo, dynamic, and style
_____ _____ Inhalation and head nod reinforces prep
_____ _____ Attack is precise and unified

TWO-COUNT PREPARATION

Yes   No

_____ _____ Preparatory position suitable for the prep beats to follow
_____ _____ Preparatory beats executed in an appropriate direction
_____ _____ First prep beat neutral—no response—but in tempo
_____ _____ Second prep beat active and in tempo, dynamic, and style of music
_____ _____ Group attack is precise

learning module FIVE

Divided Meters

OVERVIEW

In this module, you are instructed to conduct divided patterns in simple and compound meters. The module also explains traditional and effective applications of beat division in relation to major pattern counts.

CONDUCTING DIVIDED METER

▶ **COMPETENCY 7**
Demonstrate beat divisions in simple and compound meters

A conductor should conduct beats rather than attempt to beat out the rhythm of notes, even in the slowest tempos. Therefore, you should resort to divided patterns only when the tempo is too slow to maintain a steady, regular flow of the main counts.

Instruction

Employ divided patterns to achieve clarity and intensity of rhythmic flow for slow movements and traditional *adagio* introductions, and for passages where the tempo slows gradually *(ritardando)* or suddenly *(ritenuto)*. As a general rule, consider beat division when the metronome marking approaches 50.

To conduct divisions, keep the shape of the basic pattern but beat two counts at each beat point for simple meters and three counts at each beat point for compound meters. Make use of longer strokes to emphasize main beats, and use shorter, lighter strokes for subordinate beats. Think "hit-tap," using only your wrist to define the subordinate divisions. You can also clarify the pattern by turning the right wrist slightly in the direction of lateral beating, and by turning the wrist in the middle of the measure to emphasize the direction of change and the natural secondary accent (see the pattern diagrams, Figure 5-1).

Use one count of the smallest unit you are actually beating as the preparatory beat for divided meter.

FIGURE 5-1
Divided Patterns

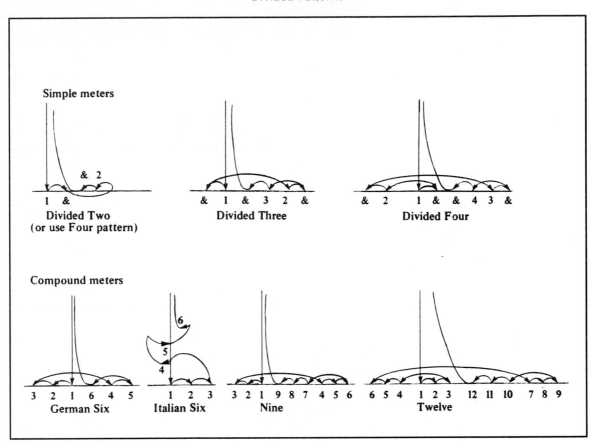

When the tempo slows gradually or abruptly, you must often divide beats for clarity. The patterns seen in Figure 5-2 seem easier to slip into from the slowing and gradually self-emphasizing rebounds in simple meter. They are most suitable for staccato and marcato passages, because they tend to be too angular to express legato style.

FIGURE 5-2
Divided Patterns—Alternative Form for Simple Meters

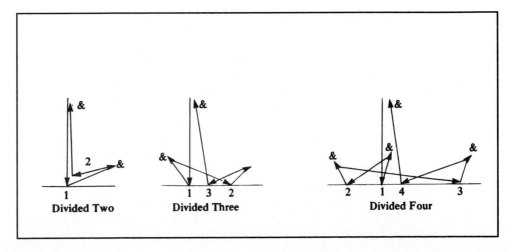

Conducting Activities

1. Practice and learn both methods for dividing simple meters. For the doubled-count approach, emphasize the major beats. For example, in divided four, think "ONE-and, TWO-and, THREE-and, FOUR-and"; or, "ONE-two, THREE-four, FIVE-six, SEVEN-eight." For the rebound approach, practice ritardandos and ritenutos in simple meters by gradually emphasizing the rebounds.

2. Practice the compound meters of six, nine, and twelve until they are automatic; emphasize the major beats. For example, in the nine meter, think "ONE-two-three, FOUR-five-six, SEVEN-eight-nine." In the six and twelve patterns, turn the right wrist position slightly in the middle of the measure to emphasize the direction of change.

3. Use a mirror to check clarity of beat and pattern. For preparation, give one count of the smallest unit you are actually beating.

4. Prepare excerpts 5-1 through 5-13 in Part III. Be ready to defend the use of the divided pattern and the method of beat division you employ.

SELF-CHECK MASTERY TEST

1. Conduct excerpts 5-1 through 5-13 in Part III, as requested by the instructor, in class with the videocassette recorder.

2. Rate your performance by using the following checklist.

DIVIDED PATTERNS

Yes	No	
——	——	Beats are well defined; ictus is clear
——	——	Appropriate preparatory beat used
——	——	Beats are in tempo, even and steady
——	——	Pattern is appropriate for music
——	——	Pattern is clear and well defined; subordinate divisions given with wrist
——	——	Pattern reflects dynamics and style of music
——	——	Musicians respond to beat, tempo, dynamics, and style

Conducting Musical Styles

OVERVIEW

A competent conductor must do more than beat time. He or she must interpret the music, reflecting in gesture the style, expression, and dynamics of the score. The basic thesis of this module is that the conductor should retain the standard beat patterns for the sake of clarity, but imbue them with expressive qualities by modifying the connecting gestures between beats.

STYLES OF BEATING

▶ *COMPETENCY 8*
Demonstrate styles of beating, including the legato, staccato, marcato, tenuto, and neutral (nonexpressive) beat styles

Your conducting must "look like" the music. Since the beat is but a point in time (as a snap of the fingers at beat points), you can achieve style and expression only by changing the character of your gestures between the beats. You may, for example, change the connection or disconnection, length, intensity, lightness or heaviness, position, and level of your beating. These gestures in combination can portray the style of the music.

Instruction

Legato   *Legato* is a smooth, sustained, connected style. You conduct it with flowing, curved gestures that connect the points of beat in the meter pattern. Move the baton slowly between beats with appropriate length and tension for the music being performed. Although the baton's movements are connected and smooth, use a subtle flick of the wrist to define the exact point of beat.

Staccato   *Staccato* is a detached, distinct style, usually indicated by a staccato mark (dot) above each shortened note. To achieve this separation in conducting, you should flick the baton quickly from beat to beat in relatively straight lines, stopping momentarily on each count. The staccato beat is usually light in character. You can depict lightness by beating a small pattern with the wrist only, without

31

tension, with little rebound, and at a high level. Some staccato passages are heavier and fuller in quality. Conduct louder, more vigorous staccato music using larger patterns, with more weight and rebound, while separating each count.

Marcato   *Marcato* is also a separated style (literally, "marked"), but it is heavier, louder, and stressed more than staccato. A series of accent marks (>) usually indicates marcato passages. Beat a larger pattern on a lower plane, with heaviness and tension. Hammer weight into it without much rebound. The degree of separation will depend on the musical context.

Tenuto   *Tenuto* is a style characterized by the stretching of beats for emphasis rather than by dynamic accentuation. A series of tenuto marks, that is, a line over each note, can signify the tenuto style (although the marks have erroneously come to be seen as signifying legato). Conduct with smoothness, intensity, weight, and slow movement between beats to stretch the notes. The true tenuto style, as contrasted with the connected legato, requires a slight separation of beats. The notes are unaccented and fully sustained with tension, yet they are slightly detached. Use a quick baton dip to effect the separation. Figure 6-1 depicts this process.

Neutral   The *neutral* or passive style lacks expressive quality and intensity. Conduct short, straight, connected lines without forearm tension to define the meter pattern. This nonexpressive beat is effective for neutral backgrounds, where the important job of the conductor is to maintain precision in the accompaniment. Passive gestures are also used to mark time during tutti rests, since no response is desired from performers. An active preparation at the end of such periods signals the resumption of the music. In a similar way, you should use neutral gestures for any extra, preliminary counts that may precede a preparatory beat, to guard against premature entrances.

FIGURE 6-1
The Tenuto with Separation

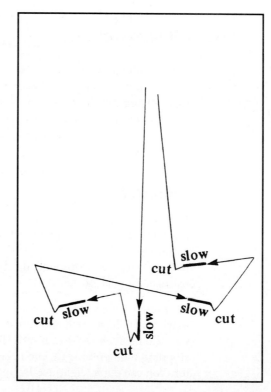

FIGURE 6-2
Quarter-Note Style Check

Conducting Activities

1. Practice the five basic styles of beating, using the appropriate preparatory gesture for each. Check your style patterns and preparations in the mirror.

2. Have your colleagues play or sing quarter notes on a predetermined pitch as you conduct the styles to see if they can read your stick. Do not show them the music or tell them what you are conducting. Vary the order of the styles you beat. Remember, your preparation must indicate the style prior to attack. Figure 6-2 shows you how to notate the styles for this quarter-note drill.

3. Prepare excerpts 6-1 through 6-10 and the following excerpts from earlier modules that exemplify the various styles: legato, 3-3, 3-12, 4-8, and 5-5; staccato, 2-13, 2-14, 4-1, 4-5, and 4-6; marcato, 2-7 and 3-2; tenuto, 2-6; and combinations, 2-4, 2-9, 3-6, and 5-2. Work to incorporate conducting styles as required by the music. Then, conduct in class with the videocassette recorder and evaluate your style patterns.

SELF-CHECK MASTERY TEST

1. Conduct excerpts 6-1 through 6-10 and other excerpts, as requested by the instructor, in class with the videocassette recorder.
2. Utilize the appropriate style pattern(s) for each composition.
3. Rate your VCR performance by using the following checklist.

CONDUCTING STYLES

Yes   No

—— ——   Preparatory beat clearly indicates style to follow
—— ——   Appropriate style(s) used and executed:
—— ——   Legato
                  Comments _____
—— ——   Staccato
                  Comments _____
—— ——   Marcato
                  Comments _____
—— ——   Tenuto
                  Comments _____
—— ——   Neutral (Nonexpressive)
                  Comments _____
—— ——   Musicians respond with requested style

learning module **SEVEN**

The Fermata

OVERVIEW

This module is designed to help you conduct compositions that include the *fermata* (hold). It provides a sound basis for solving the interpretative and conducting problems created by the various kinds of holds. The paragraphs that follow present important background information to prepare you for the conducting activities.

Definition

The fermata is usually defined as a temporary interruption or cessation in the regular flow of rhythm. Although composers have used fermatas frequently to underscore the effect of a concluding chord in a section or of a final tonic resolution, the fermata functions differently within a passage. It requires a performer to stretch a note long enough to create stress or tension by thwarting our expectation of continuing movement. It is more than an interruption; it is an expressive device.

Interpretation

You should always think of the fermata expressively, in terms of its agogic function. It is a climactic, prolonged, and highly tensional focal point in the musical line. Such factors as phrase shape, fermata location, form, style, and tradition determine the appropriate method of execution. You must consider all three parts of a fermata in order to guide your interpretation and develop your manual technique: attack, duration, and termination.

Attack Remember that the fermata begins at a point of beat (or in some instances at a fractional part of beat). You must move the baton directly to that point in the pattern at the appropriate tempo, as if the fermata were not there. Do not hesitate or fail to provide an ictus (wrist flick) for a precise attack.

Duration The length of the fermata and the intensity of tone depend on structural and historical context. Conductors must base their final interpretation on score study and on the feeling of rightness they have for the particular composition. To maintain intensity, you should keep the baton moving slowly with appropriate tension in the forearm. If the fermata is to be sustained for a long duration, you should also use your left hand, thumbside up, palm at an upward angle, to support the dynamic level.

Termination Context also determines the way you should terminate the hold. The fermata at the end of a section or before a rest must be released. For a long pause after the hold, the release must be followed by an independent preparatory beat. The fermata at the end of a phrase is usually given a phrasing gesture. Here the release motion also functions as a preparatory beat. A fermata within a phrase or with a leading, upbeat quality is usually not released, but requires a preparatory gesture to restart the rhythmic flow. As a competent conductor, you must master all three possible types of termination.

FERMATA WITH CAESURA

▶ ***COMPETENCY 9.1***
Demonstrate the fermata, with a release and caesura of appropriate length, and subsequent preparatory beat

You should stop the group after a fermata (1) when the fermata ends a section, (2) when it precedes a rest, and (3) when it requires a caesura (///), that is, a complete break that is written or implied. To interpret correctly, you must use two separate gestures: one to release the hold and, after a period of silence, another to prepare the next entrance.

Instruction

Follow these steps to conduct the fermata with caesura:

1. Move directly into the hold.
2. Sustain it for an appropriate length with proper tension.
3. Give a release gesture; decide in advance where you want to stop your baton after the cutoff so that you will be in position to give a preparatory beat for the next count of music.
4. After a suitable duration of silence (motionless baton), conduct the preparatory beat. Give it as if you are starting a new piece. It must indicate tempo, dynamic level, and style. (See Figure 7-1.)

FERMATA WITH BREATH PAUSE

▶ ***COMPETENCY 9.2***
Demonstrate the fermata, with the release gesture used as a preparatory beat

When the hold requires a breath after the release, you should use a breathing or phrasing gesture. Here the cutoff also serves as a preparatory beat. This release/prep motion consists of one extra beat in tempo. That is, the count of the hold is given a second time as a cutoff, and the baton motion continues upward as a preparation during the one-count period of silence. The cut/prep gesture must also indicate the tempo, dynamic level, and style of the music that follows it.

FIGURE 7-1
Fermata with Caesura

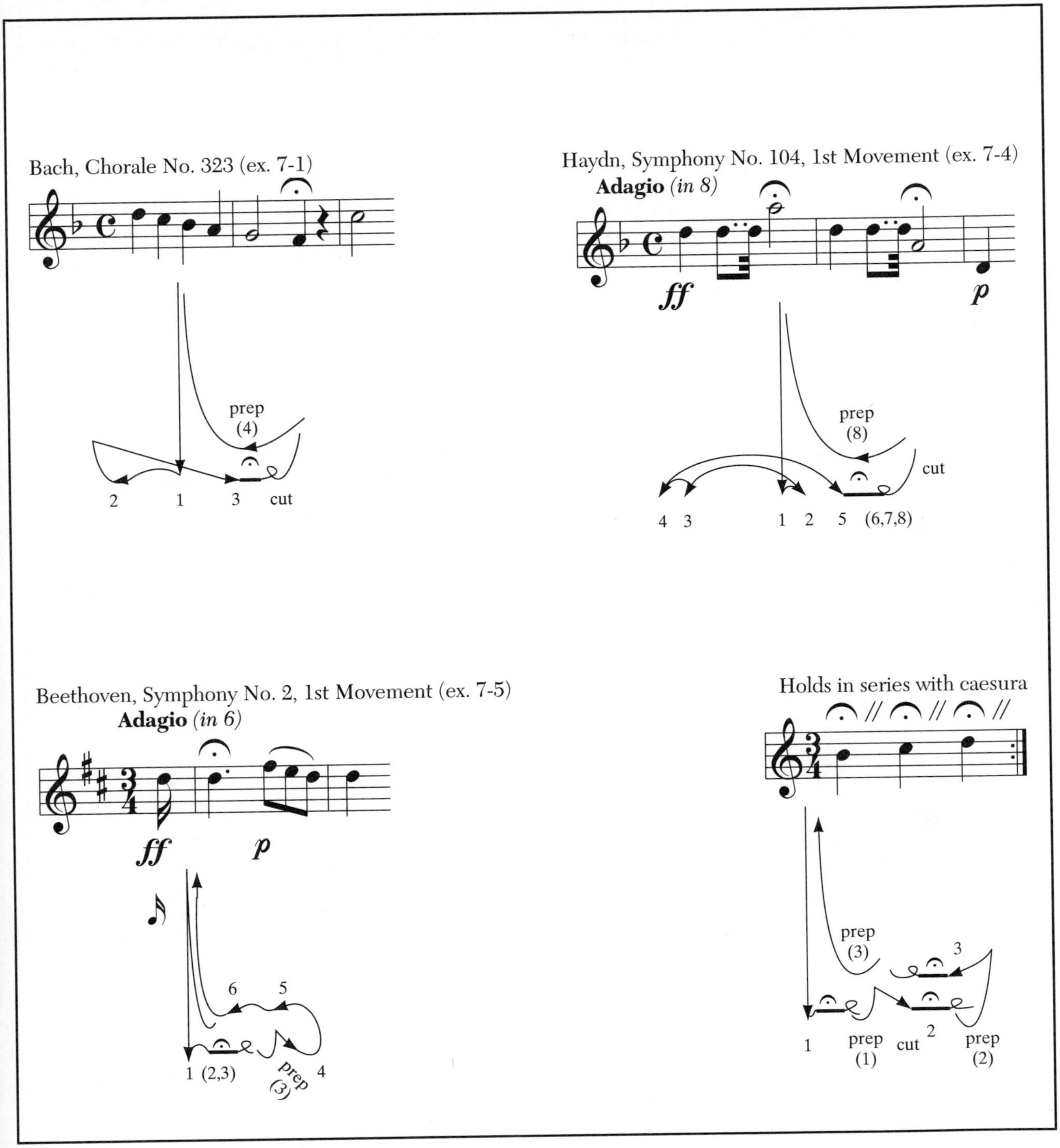
Bach, Chorale No. 323 (ex. 7-1)
prep
(4)
2 1 3 cut
Haydn, Symphony No. 104, 1st Movement (ex. 7-4)
Adagio (in 8)
ff
p
prep
(8)
cut
4 3 1 2 5 (6,7,8)
Beethoven, Symphony No. 2, 1st Movement (ex. 7-5)
Adagio (in 6)
ff
p
6 5
1 (2,3)
prep
(3)
4
Holds in series with caesura
prep
(3)
3
1
prep
(1)
cut
2
prep
(2)

Instruction

Follow these steps to execute the fermata with breath release:

1. Move directly into the hold.
2. Sustain it for an appropriate length.

FIGURE 7-2
Fermata with Breath Pause

National Anthem (ex. 7-18)

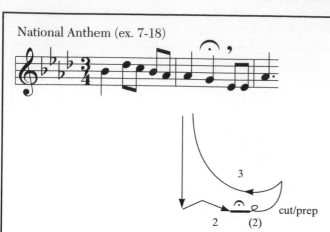

Herbert, "I Want What I Want" (ex. 7-19)

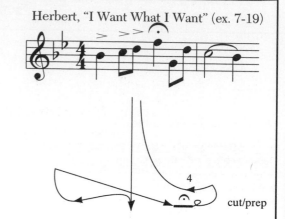

Bach, Chorale No. 172 (ex. 7-3)

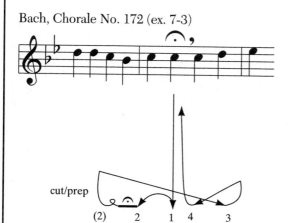

Ives-Schuman, *Variations on "America"* (ex. 7-9)
(in 2)

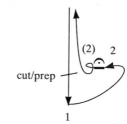

© Copyright 1949, 1964 and 1968 by Merion Music, Inc.
Used by permission of Theodore Presser Company

Holds in series with breath pause
The cut-off serves as the preparation

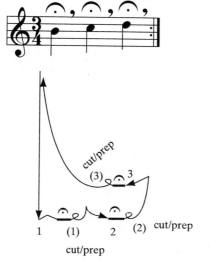

3. Give a release gesture that swings up to function as a one-count preparatory beat for the following entrance. Breathe in during this upward swing. Keep the baton in tempo and move without hesitation into the next count of the meter pattern where the music resumes. (See Figure 7-2.)

FERMATA WITHOUT RELEASE

▶ ***COMPETENCY 9.3***
Demonstrate the fermata, without release but with a preparatory gesture to signal resumption

You usually do not release a fermata when it is located within a phrase or when it is used expressively to lead into another note, phrase, or section. However, you must give a preparatory motion to indicate resumption. This gesture should be either a one-count or a half-count preparation, depending on the tempo of the music that follows. Watch that you do not make a jerky prep motion, or the musicians will release. Just lift up smoothly in tempo and use your left hand to signal connection.

Instruction

Follow these steps to execute the nonreleased fermata:

1. Move directly into the hold.
2. Sustain it for an appropriate length.
3. Swing up smoothly for a one or one-half count resumption gesture. It must not look like a release. Use the left hand in a sustaining gesture during the right-hand preparation. (See Figure 7-3.)

Conducting Activities

1. Practice holds on each count of all meters in each of the three types of termination. Remember that all first counts are the same—down. All last counts are also the same—across to the left. For every fermata on the last count in any meter, move the baton horizontally to the left across the body rather than upwardly. This puts you in position to swing up for the preparatory beat. (See Figure 7-4.)

2. When practicing the fermata in the various patterns, you may find it helpful to count the beats out loud, repeating the beat number of the hold for the preparatory beat (or gesture of resumption). Thus, a fermata on the beat of three in a four pattern would be counted "one-two-threeeee-three-four," etc., where the repeated number indicates first the beat held and then the preparatory beat.

3. Prepare a "quarter-note drill" using the three types of fermatas to check the clarity of your gestures. To create this drill, write out a series of quarter notes using several meters with holds of different types on various counts (see Figure 7-5 for an example). The purpose of this exercise is to elicit the desired response from the performers by means of gesture alone. They should not see the music. Use a mirror for initial practice. Then, ask a fellow musician to respond to your conducting by playing or singing quarter notes on one pitch. Your colleague's hesitations and false starts will give clues as to possible conducting problems. If he or she does

FIGURE 7-3
Fermata without Release

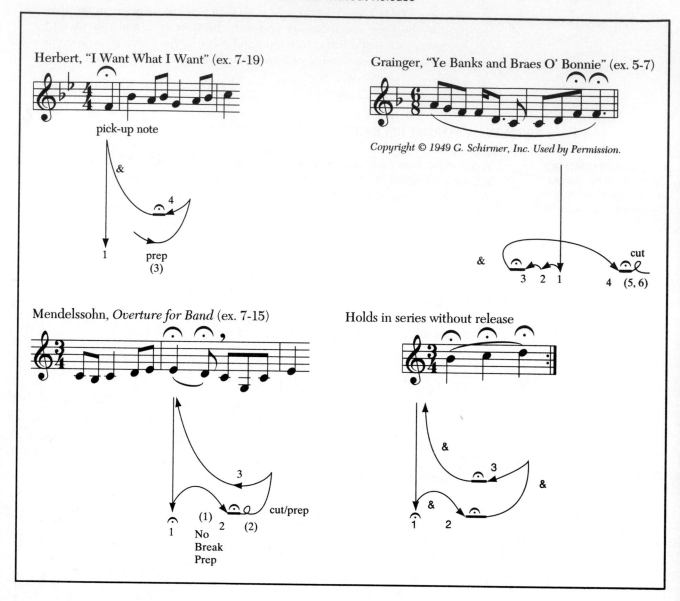

Herbert, "I Want What I Want" (ex. 7-19)

pick-up note

&

4

1

prep
(3)

Grainger, "Ye Banks and Braes O' Bonnie" (ex. 5-7)

Copyright © 1949 G. Schirmer, Inc. Used by Permission.

&

3 2 1

cut

4 (5, 6)

Mendelssohn, *Overture for Band* (ex. 7-15)

3

1

(1)

2

(2)

cut/prep

No
Break
Prep

Holds in series without release

&

3

&

1

&

2

FIGURE 7-4
Consistency of Holds on First and Last Counts

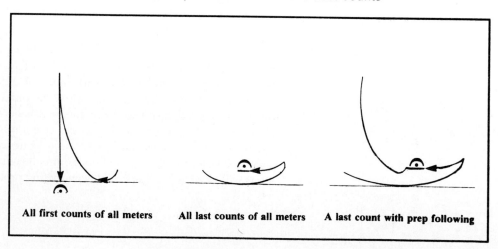

All first counts of all meters   **All last counts of all meters**   **A last count with prep following**

FIGURE 7-5
Sample Quarter-Note Drill for the Fermata

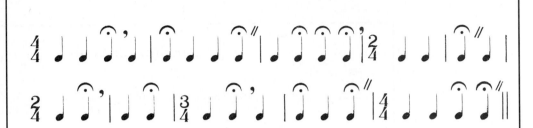

⌢" = release and break (motionless baton) with a subsequent, independent preparatory beat

⌢' = cut/prep, phrasing beat (baton motion continues since the release gesture becomes the preparatory beat)

⌢ = no break, with a one-half count resumption gesture

not respond correctly to what you are conducting, ask for an opinion as to what is wrong with your gestures. Show your quarter-note drill to your colleague and ask if he or she thinks that your conducting agrees with the notation.

4. Conduct the class through a quarter-note drill to determine if the group can follow your gestures. Check your performance by using the videocassette recorder.

5. Analyze, prepare, and practice excerpts 7-1 through 7-23 in Part III. Use the appropriate interpretation and type of hold indicated by the musical context. Note that more than one interpretation may be acceptable. Be prepared to justify your choice. Conduct the class, then evaluate your performance by using the VCR checklist provided in this module.

SELF-CHECK MASTERY TEST

1. Demonstrate the fermata on all beats and division of beats in all meters as requested by your instructor.
   a. With release and subsequent preparatory beat
   b. With release used as a preparatory beat
   c. Without release but with a preparatory gesture

2. Lead the class through a quarter-note drill that you devise. Include various meters with holds of different types on various counts. To determine if the group can follow, only you and the instructor should have the music. Perform this drill on a predetermined pitch.

3. Conduct the excerpts from Part III requested by your instructor, in class with the videocassette recorder. Use the appropriate types of holds required by each example.

4. Rate your VCR performance by using the following checklist.

CONDUCTING FERMATAS

Yes   No

____ ____ Fermatas clearly and correctly executed; e.g., attacked directly, sustained, terminated appropriately

____ ____ Baton moves slowly with intensity to maintain tone
Comments _____

____ ____ Length appropriate
Comments _____

____ ____ Releases concise, in style and dynamic level of music
Comments _____

____ ____ Preparatory beats clear and in the tempo, dynamic level, and style of music
Comments _____

____ ____ Cut/prep, breathing beat used appropriately and executed properly
Comments _____

____ ____ If no release, resumption indicated by an anticipatory motion of one or one-half count in tempo
Comments _____

____ ____ Left hand used for support
Comments _____

learning module **EIGHT**

The Cue

OVERVIEW

This module instructs you to cue entrances of sections or individuals for precision of attack, dynamic level, style, and expression. You will learn three methods for giving cues and when to use each of them.

CUING GESTURES

▶ **COMPETENCY 10**
Demonstrate cuing gestures with the left hand, baton, and nod of head, with eye contact and preparation for each

Cuing provides assurance for entering players or singers and achieves unity of entrances. To be effective, cues must be prepared. Your cue preparation should signal "ready—begin" in the tempo, dynamic level, and style of the oncoming passage. You can cue with the left hand, the baton, or the head. Determine the type of cue to use by the character of the music, the location of the musicians being cued, and the number of instruments or parts entering. Eye contact is essential for all cues. Look at the entering performers before and during the cue.

Instruction

Left-hand cue   To execute the basic left-hand cue, you should signal the entering performers by pointing at them with the index finger of the left hand. However, merely pointing at performers at the moment of entrance is an inefficient and unnerving gesture. To achieve a unified entrance, you must look at them and prepare the cue with an upswing that indicates the kind of attack, dynamic level, style, and expression you desire. Since finger pointing may become overused, you should employ variations of the basic left-hand gesture to fit the music—the clenched fist for force, the palm facing the musicians for softness or balance, the palm facing your chest for warmth or expression, the open hand outstretched with palm upward for free, open responses, or a wide, sweeping motion with the arm for large, full entrances. As a general rule, you should reserve left-hand cues for important entrances of many parts and for individuals located at your extreme left.

Baton cue   To give the baton cue, face and look at the incoming musicians, and point the baton in their direction as you incorporate the preparatory gesture and entrance beat into the regular conducting pattern. You should keep the beat pattern intact while advancing the baton in the direction of the performers being cued. This cue is effective for most situations. Use it frequently for all entrances except for performers at your extreme left.

Head cue   To effect a head cue, look at the players or singers, and give an up-down, ready-go motion of the chin. With eye contact and breathing, the well-timed nod of the head toward an incoming soloist or section is the most subtle, effective device for individual and small section entrances.

For several, scattered, simultaneous entrances give a nondirectional cue for them all, or cue the largest incoming group. If many parts are entering in close succession, do not attempt to cue, but do maintain a good, clear beat and pattern. Always encourage your group to count rests. A cue should provide support but never replace the meticulous counting of rests by performers.

Conducting Activities

1. Mentally visualize the location of the various sections of your group and practice bringing in soloists and sections on different counts of various meters, using each type of cue.

2. Prepare excerpts 8-1 through 8-8 in Part III and incorporate cuing gestures. Carefully decide which method you will use for each cued part. Be ready to justify your choice when you conduct in class.

SELF-CHECK MASTERY TEST ━━━━━━━━━━━━━━━━━━━━━━━━━━━━━━

1. Conduct excerpts 8-1 through 8-8, as requested by the instructor, in class with the videocassette recorder.

2. Use the three types of cues as appropriate.

3. Provide a rationale for your choice of cues, if asked.

4. Rate your VCR performance by using the following checklist.

CUING

Yes	No	
____	____	Sufficient cues given
____	____	Appropriate cues given
____	____	Cues given clearly and with facility
____	____	Cues prepared
____	____	Cues in correct tempo, dynamic level, and style
____	____	Cues given with left hand
____	____	Cues given with baton
____	____	Cues given with nod of head (chin)
____	____	Eye contact secured and maintained through the count of cue

The Left Hand

OVERVIEW

The purpose of this module is to develop your left hand into a functional, autonomous, and expressive conducting instrument. Although you may use the left hand on occasion to mirror and reinforce the right hand in patterns, fermatas, preparations, and releases, it must become rhythmically independent for cuing, shaping phrases, giving crescendos, balancing parts, and the like.

LEFT-HAND GESTURES

▶ **COMPETENCY 11**
Demonstrate independent and effective use of the left hand to signal dynamics, subito changes, accents, phrasing, and balance

Ambidexterity is necessary for the conductor, and you must work for it continuously. The commonplace task of turning pages of the score while maintaining the beat, the conducting pattern, and the style of beating illustrates the problem well, and provides you with a good beginning practice exercise. Although you may mirror beat patterns for emphasis and clarity, you can make the best use of the left hand by using independent, expressive gestures. In general, the right hand serves as a technician, whereas the left hand functions as an interpreter. In this artistic capacity, the left hand gives phrasing, dynamics, nuance, accentuation, *subito* (sudden) changes, and anything necessary to clarify and reinforce the gestures of the right hand. When it is not in use, keep the left hand close to the waist in front of the body. This is the best ready position.

Instruction

Crescendo   The crescendo mark indicates a gradual increase in loudness of tone. Thus, you may need to signal a significant drop in dynamics initially to provide a level from which to expand in volume and intensity. After beginning, be in no rush to imply loudness. Performers tend to think of crescendo as "get loud," which results in a sudden expansion ($\diagdown$) instead of a gradual feeding of intensity by

ILLUSTRATION 9-1
Conducting the Crescendo

degrees (◁═══). Indicate the crescendo by gradually lifting the left hand, thumbside up, palm at an upward angle, with increasing tension in the forearm. (See Illustration 9-1.) You must simultaneously increase the size and intensity of the right-hand beat pattern. Be certain the left hand rises smoothly, without jerking at each beat of the right hand.

Diminuendo   In contrast, a diminuendo means to diminish in loudness. Turn your palm over gradually to face the group, lowering it slowly while continuing to turn it downward (or turn it inward to the body). If you turn the palm over too quickly, performers may respond with a subito effect (▷═══) instead of the desired fading effect (═══◁).

Support dynamic levels   Use the left hand to indicate a continuing *forte* level, especially for final tones or holds, which tend to diminuendo if not supported. Hold the palm upward or inward with tension to represent continued intensity of tone. Conversely, to conduct a *sempre piano,* hold up the palm of the hand with fingers together toward the musicians, and beat a small right-hand pattern close to the body. The often photographed Toscanini "shh" position with the left index finger on the lips is another effective signal for soft passages.

Subito contrasts   To achieve subito changes in dynamics and style, you must execute an appropriate anticipatory gesture on the rebound of the preceding beat to signal the desired change. Remember, *all subito changes must be prepared on the preceding rebound, that is, on the "and."* For example, making a clenched fist on the rebound portends a sudden accent or forceful attack.

ILLUSTRATION 9-2
Conducting the *Subito Piano*

Subito **fp.** To signal a *subito forte* to *piano,* quickly pull back the left hand to your chest so the palm faces the performers. (See Illustration 9-2.) Do this on the rebound preceding the beat of change. Then, beat a small light pattern.

Subito **pf.** To conduct a *subito piano* to *forte,* make a fist on the rebound and simultaneously enlarge the size and intensity of the right-hand beat pattern. (See Illustration 9-3.) Figure 9-1 shows how subito changes of dynamics can be achieved.

Subito *legato.* To effect the sudden legato style, make a smooth, connected gesture on the rebound while simultaneously indicating the appropriate dynamic level.

Subito *staccato.* Execute the *subito-piano* staccato by lightly flicking and pulling back the left hand on the rebound, accompanied by a sudden high, light, small, and separated right-hand pattern.

Subito *marcato.* To move to a *subito-forte* marcato, make a fist with the left hand (coupled with tension in the forearm) on the rebound, and begin a sudden large, low, heavy beat pattern in the right hand.

Accents   Give accents in a manner similar to that used in conducting the subito marcato, since they also must be prepared. Signal the accent on the preceding rebound with a clenched fist gesture, using appropriate tension and beat weight for the strength of the accent. Remember that an accent is usually one dynamic level louder than its surrounding context.

Syncopation and offbeat accents   Offbeat accents are prepared differently. In syncopated figures and other offbeat attacks, you execute the preparatory motion

ILLUSTRATION 9-3
Conducting the *Subito Forte*

FIGURE 9-1
Subito Changes of Dynamics

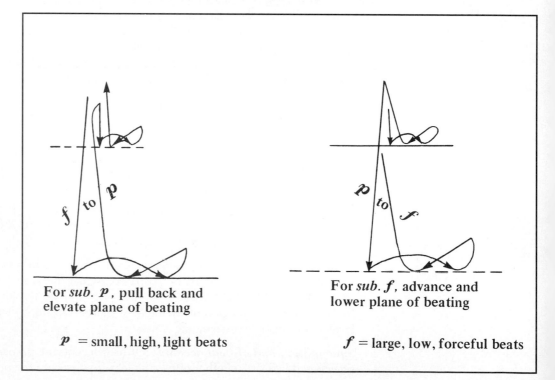

For *sub.* *p*, pull back and
elevate plane of beating

p = small, high, light beats

For *sub.* *f*, advance and
lower plane of beating

f = large, low, forceful beats

on the beat (*not* on the rebound) to assure that the reaction of the musicians occurs precisely at the offbeat. Remember, the best thing you can do to secure a good offbeat is to conduct a clear, steady beat. Do not attempt to give the offbeat accents by dividing the pattern, especially at faster tempos. Since response can only follow a gesture, it is futile to expect musicians to perform simultaneously with your divisions. Such divisions are often disruptive to the rhythmic flow, as in the case of the choir director who conducts words instead of beats and phrases.

Phrase and phrasing beat   Use the left hand to help the right hand pull and shape the phrase contour. Build intensity and movement by using an expanding upward motion with tension. Feel the rise in intensity and the subsequent falling away of tension to cadence. Give a phrasing gesture (baton dip) to end the phrase and then swing up from it for a breath. In choral music, you must give a precise release gesture at the end of a phrase to assure precision of ensemble and clarity of the final consonant. Execute the phrasing gesture as you would the cut/prep motion used for certain fermatas (see Figure 9-2). This may momentarily break the tempo, as in a *rubato* (consult Module Eleven for an explanation and interpretation of rubato). Reinforce the phrasing beat with the left hand by giving a wrist flick or by bringing your fingers against your thumb for release. Conversely, use the left hand to smooth over places where the players want to let down intensity or breathe, breaking the phrase. You may resort to continuous circular motions or arc-like gestures with upward intensity (⌒).

Nuance   Nuance refers to subtle expressive, dynamic, and agogic shading within the phrase, either written (**< >**) or implied. It is on a much smaller scale than an out-and-out crescendo to a diminuendo. Conduct this subtle effect with the left hand and wrist only, without arm movement, by slightly raising the palm and slowly turning the hand over.

Balance   The left hand balances parts by signaling dynamic adjustments and alterations. To bring out an important melodic line, give the performers an encouraging look while moving the index finger in a come-forth gesture. To subdue a loud group, face the offending musicians with palm out toward them and give them a severe look or shake your head.

FIGURE 9-2
Phrasing Gesture

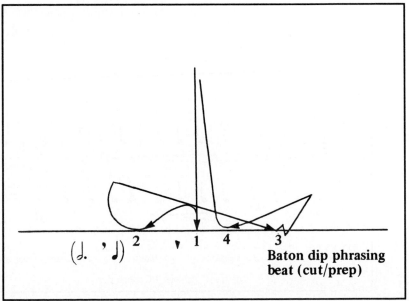

Conducting Activities

1. If you have trouble using your hands independently, practice keeping a steady beat and consistent pattern while turning pages of a score or a book, or while engaging in other activities.

2. Practice giving a crescendo and diminuendo while maintaining a steady beat in various meters. Keep the left-hand gestures smooth with proper tension, not jerking with the beat gestures. Think of feeding the crescendo by degrees, perhaps counting one *(ppp)* through ten *(fff)*. Adjust the size and intensity of the beat pattern to the dynamic level.

3. Practice giving subito dynamic and style changes, such as *forte-marcato* to *piano-staccato*, at two-measure intervals. Use various meter patterns and keep the tempo steady. Execute the required anticipatory gesture on the preceding rebound.

4. Give accents on predetermined counts in various meters. Employ the needed preparation.

5. Practice sustaining and supporting a final *forte* tone with the left hand.

6. Practice giving nuance and phrasing with the left hand. Indicate phrase endings by a baton dip for quick release and a fractional preparatory (breathe in) gesture for resumption. Reinforce the release with the left hand.

7. Prepare quarter-note drills in several meters, incorporating various changes in dynamics and style. Figure 9-3 and the drill in Appendix B provide examples. Use a mirror for initial practice. Then have fellow musicians respond to your conducting to determine if your gestures are clear and properly timed. Check subito preparations especially. Performers will make the subito change one count late if you wait to signal it *on* the beat rather than prepare it *before* the beat during the prior rebound. They will respond a count or more early if you prepare too soon.

8. Study excerpts 9-1 through 9-18, incorporating left-hand signals and gestures into the scores as appropriate.

FIGURE 9-3
Sample Quarter-Note Drill

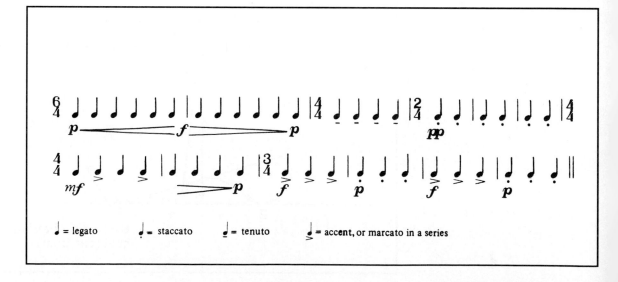

SELF-CHECK MASTERY TEST _____

1. Lead the class through a quarter-note drill that you devise. Include the crescendo, diminuendo, accents, and subito changes of dynamics and style.

2. Conduct excerpts from Part III, as requested by the instructor, in class with the videocassette recorder. Demonstrate independent use of hands by incorporating and executing effective left-hand gestures in each excerpt.

3. Rate your VCR performance by using the following checklist.

LEFT-HAND TECHNIQUE

Yes   No

____ ____ Left hand is independent of right; does more than mirror gestures
Comments _____

____ ____ Crescendo given
Comments _____

____ ____ Diminuendo given
Comments _____

____ ____ Subito changes of dynamics given
Comments _____

____ ____ Subito changes of style given
Comments _____

____ ____ Accents given
Comments _____

____ ____ Tones supported, especially holds and final tones
Comments _____

____ ____ Parts balanced
Comments _____

____ ____ Nuances indicated
Comments _____

____ ____ Phrasing given; rise-fall, climax
Comments _____

_____ Phrasing beat used
Comments _____

Asymmetrical and Changing Meters

| OVERVIEW

This module requires you to conduct uneven and changing meters in slow and fast tempos. Mastery of the techniques and principles contained in the module will enable you to perform much of the contemporary repertory.

CONDUCTING UNEVEN AND CHANGING METERS

► *COMPETENCY 12*

Demonstrate changing meters and asymmetrical patterns in slow and fast tempos

Contemporary composers often write music with uneven meters that shift in rapid succession to disturb or displace the normal and expected regularity of beats. Although the effect may be nonmetric for a listener, the conductor and musicians must keep the beat or a division of the beat steady for unity of performance.

Instruction

Beating five and seven To conduct asymmetrical meters, you should use variations of the regular, even patterns. To beat five, use a four pattern but insert one extra count in the appropriate place; or use a six pattern and delete one count. Conduct seven by using a divided three pattern and adding the extra beat as required. You must always analyze the music to determine how beats are grouped by secondary accent, and then adjust your patterns to the metric accentuations (see Figure 10-1).

Changing meters When music shifts from meter to meter but maintains a constant basic beat, you simply conduct a steady beat and change the pattern for each of the successive meters ($\frac{4}{4}$ ♩ ♩ ♩ ♩ | $\frac{2}{4}$ ♩ ♩ | $\frac{3}{4}$ ♩ ♩ ♩ | $\frac{4}{4}$ ♩ ♩ ♩ ♩ | etc.). However, if some meters are asymmetrical, you may have to adjust the speed of

FIGURE 10-1
Asymmetrical Patterns of Five and Seven with Common Groupings

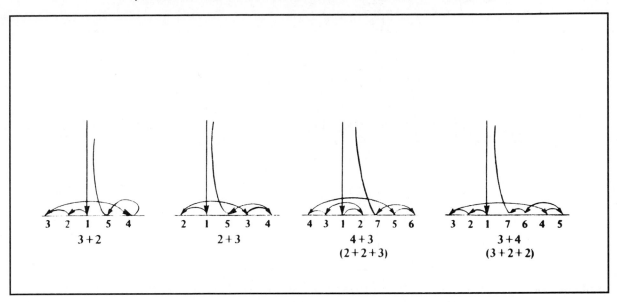

the patterns. For example, occasional three-eight measures interspersed within a composition are traditionally conducted at twice the tempo. The eighth-note division remains constant. Beat a small three pattern with the wrist only for such double-time measures (see Figure 10-2).

However, such eighth notes should be subsumed within a larger beat structure when the tempo is too fast to beat double time clearly. As Figure 10-3 shows, you should beat the three-eight measures in one because of the allegro tempo. Since an eighth note equals an eighth note throughout, be careful not to conduct the three eighth notes as triplets.

FIGURE 10-2
Beating Out Double Time for Certain Three-Eight Measures

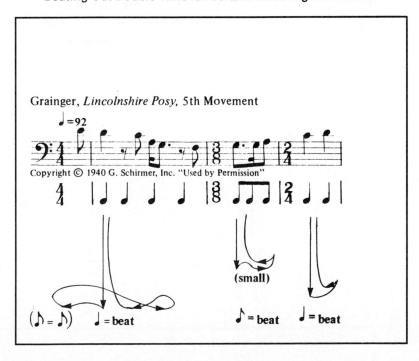

FIGURE 10-3
Beating Three-Eight Measures in One

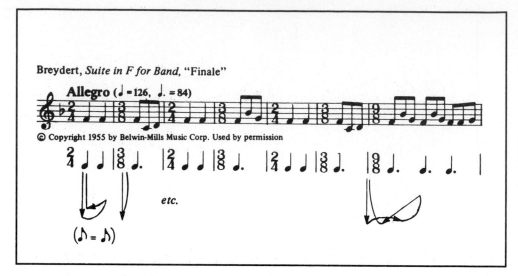

Uneven patterns When tempos are fast, conduct asymmetrical meters with uneven or lopsided beat patterns. The division of the beat, usually the eighth note, must remain constant, so you must vary the speed between beats to maintain the consistent beat division. That is, you hasten or you drag the beat rebound to accommodate the uneven beats that make up the lopsided patterns. This technique is illustrated in Figure 10-4.

You may find it helpful to use a system of counting that incorporates the extra division as an additional "and." For five-eight meter with a division of 2 + 3, count "one-and, two-and-and"; for a division of 3 + 2, count "one-and-and, two-and." In seven-eight meter divided 2 + 2 + 3, count "one-and, two-and, three-and-and"; for a 3 + 2 + 2 division, count "one-and-and, two-and, three-and," and so on. (See Figure 10-5.)

FIGURE 10-4
Beating Lopsided Patterns of Five-Eight and Seven-Eight

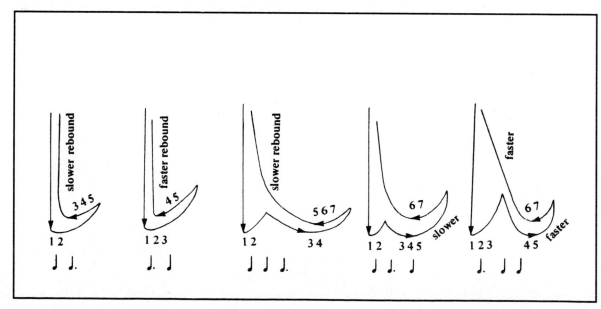

FIGURE 10-5
Counting with an Extra "And"

Secondary accents may fall differently in any meter, creating an asymmetrical effect. For example, nine-eight meter may be written 2 + 2 + 2 + 3 (♫ ♫ ♫ ♫♫), in which case you must conduct a four pattern with a slower speed on the fourth count. Eight-eight meter may be written 3 + 3 + 2 (♫♫ ♫♫ ♫). Here you conduct a three pattern with a faster speed on the third count.

Note: A single preparation is sufficient for the lopsided patterns. Make certain that the preparatory beat is exactly the time value of the *first count* of music performed, not the last count of the lopsided measure, since musicians catch their initial beat length from the tempo of the preparation. See Figure 10-6 for some examples.

Conducting Activities

1. Practice the five and seven patterns with their various secondary accents.
2. Practice shifting from meter to meter keeping beat notes steady.
3. Practice uneven meters with lopsided patterns, varying the secondary accents and keeping the division equal. If you have trouble keeping divisions steady and even, tap the equal divisions with your left hand while conducting lopsided patterns with your right hand. Then, use a metronome set to the beat division to give you the most exacting and disciplined practice. Be sure to speed up or slow down the speed of the

FIGURE 10-6
Preparatory Beats for Uneven Meter Patterns

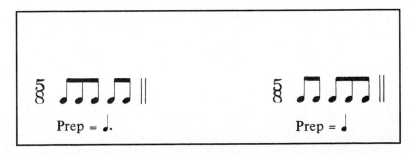

baton between major beats to accommodate the varying number of even beat divisions. See Appendix E for practice in counting drills for selected excerpts.

4. Prepare excerpts 10-1 through 10-22 in Part III. Incorporate appropriate patterns and preparations for the tempo and style of music.

SELF-CHECK MASTERY TEST

1. Conduct excerpts 10-1 through 10-22 as requested by the instructor, in class with the videocassette recorder.

2. Rate your VCR performance by using the following checklist.

UNEVEN AND CHANGING BEAT PATTERNS

Yes   No

_____ _____ Preparatory beat is appropriate
Comments _____

_____ _____ Beats are well defined; the ictus occurs precisely at major beat points in lopsided patterns
Comments _____

_____ _____ Divisions remain constant
Comments _____

_____ _____ Secondary accents are given correctly
Comments _____

_____ _____ Patterns are appropriate, clear, and well defined
Comments _____

_____ _____ Musicians respond exactly to beat pulsations
Comments _____

---

learning module **ELEVEN**

Tempo Changes and Accompanying

OVERVIEW

This module will teach you to lead the group through gradual and sudden tempo modifications while maintaining ensemble unity and precision. A famous conductor once quipped that his job was really not too difficult: "You must give a good preparatory beat to get the musicians started together, and then be sure you stop when they do!" The humor contains an element of truth from the musicians' viewpoint. A conductor is hardly needed in many compositions after he or she establishes the tempo. For example, once you start a march, you can stop conducting altogether without doing too much harm to the performance. However, players depend most on a conductor's strong leadership when the tempo changes suddenly or fluctuates gradually as in transitional passages and accompaniments.

CONDUCTING TEMPO VARIATIONS

▶ *COMPETENCY 13*
Demonstrate gradual and subito changes in tempo and the ability to accompany

Beat size is related to tempo as well as dynamics. Use smaller patterns for faster and softer music, and larger patterns for slower and louder music. Obviously, you must make adjustments to fit specific compositions. For example, put more intensity into a small pattern for loud, fast music; and use a small pattern with a slower velocity between beats for soft, slow compositions. As a general rule for tempo change, make the size of your beats *smaller* as you speed up the tempo and make them *larger* when you slow down the tempo. You may find this contrary to your natural instincts, but it will eliminate much needless and ineffective flailing.

Instruction

As in all effective conducting, tempo changes must be prepared. You execute these preparations most often on the preceding rebound or on a series of after-beats.

Ritardando and ritenuto   To bring about a *ritardando,* gradually increase the size of the beat pattern while slowing the speed of the baton between beats. That is, concentrate on slowing the rebounds for preparation; the beats will take care of themselves. For a *ritenuto,* you must suddenly slow or stretch the offbeat preparation immediately preceding the ritenuto measure and simultaneously increase the size of beats.

Accelerando   To accelerate the tempo, gradually increase the speed between beats for preparation and conduct a pattern of decreasing size. In a long accelerando, you may be required to switch into a pattern of fewer beats to accommodate the faster tempo. This often occurs in Viennese waltzes and other triple meters where the three pattern shifts to one. (The reverse will happen at a ritardando or allargando.) The *Egmont* Overture by Beethoven has such a transition at the Allegro, measure 25. The coda, Allegro con brio, measures 286–295, requires a transition from the four to two pattern. (See Figures 11-1 and 11-2.)

Subito tempo change   You must use a subito preparatory gesture when a section within a composition requires an immediate change of tempo, for instance, the traditional adagio introduction followed by an allegro in classical style. You execute most subito tempo changes by swinging up with a half-count "and/prep" on the preceding rebound in the tempo of the change. Follow this procedure: think "and—one" in the new tempo while simultaneously putting that tempo into the prior preparatory rebound and initial downbeat with an up-down wrist action. A nod of the head helps secure the new tempo. Use the chin and your physiognomy in general. You may, of course, have the opportunity to execute a full, one-count preparatory beat for the new tempo if the original tempo is slow enough or if a rest or caesura intervenes.

Rubato   The literal translation of *rubato* from the Italian is "robbed." It refers to agogic accentuation (expressive lengthening) of important notes in the musical line, and the subsequent shortening and hastening of less important notes, which are thus "robbed" of part of their time values. For expressive conducting, you must

FIGURE 11-1
Transition from Three to One

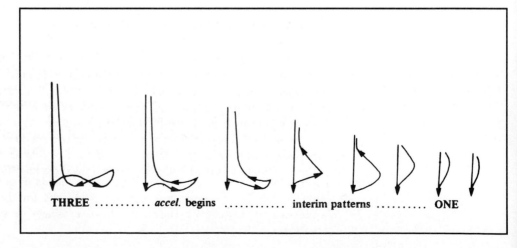

THREE .... *accel.* begins .... interim patterns .... ONE

FIGURE 11-2
Transition from Four to Two

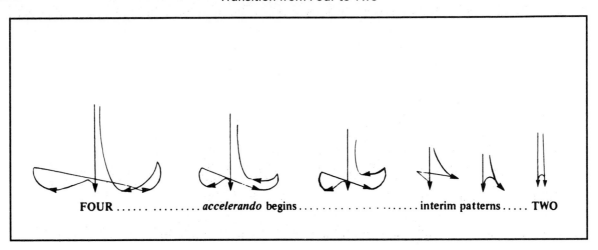

FOUR .... *accelerando* begins .... interim patterns ..... TWO

interpret two kinds of rubato: the "push-on" rubato, which drives ahead to intensify the phrase or section; and the "hanging" rubato, which holds back or hesitates to create tension. Phrase structure provides the clue to the appropriate use of each type, singly or in combination.

To conduct a push-on rubato, you slightly accelerate the tempo, just push it a little, to create agitation and intensity through forced movement to the phrase climax. Then you slacken to the original tempo for a release of tension at the cadence.

To execute the hanging rubato, hold back or stretch an important note or group of notes near the beginning of a phrase, and then make a slight accelerando to overtake the original tempo. Intensity is heightened by the initial tenuto or ritenuto. Practice rubato phrasing using Figure 11-3.

Reserve extreme rubato give-and-take for romantic music or for passages marked *espressivo* and *tempo rubato*. However, you may judiciously use the principles of rubato for subtle shading and phrasing for the majority of expressive music in all styles.

Accompaniments Conducting accompaniments requires effective preparatory gestures and the flexibility of rubato. Your primary job is to conduct the orchestra, not the soloist, although you should cue and help the soloist as needed. Practice the techniques of accompanying by conducting recitatives and cadenzas, following the free-flowing solo lines. Use recordings, especially different performances of the same recitative, to practice following the soloist.

Give clear, precise preparations and cues for entering orchestral parts, and anticipatory gestures when chords change. The timing of the preparations is critical for precision and dramatic effect. Downbeats must be clear for musicians to keep their place, especially when they enter at varying times. Patterns must also be clear when note values vary among the parts.

During long, sustained chords, beat small, neutral patterns or, perhaps, only the downbeat of each measure. Indicate dynamics, style, and balance as required. Conduct neutral downbeats only during long rests to mark the passage of measures. Many conductors give unobtrusive downbeats in quick succession to indicate the number of measures' rest, and then wait for the soloist before giving a preparatory gesture for the next entrance. Whatever system you choose, be consistent.

FIGURE 11-3
Hanging and Push-on Rubato

Practice the "hanging" rubato and the "push-on" rubato using this exercise. Play it; sing it; and conduct it. Then turn back to excerpt 9-4, relating the feel for the two types of phrase movement to the musical context.

Vaughan Williams, *English Folksong Suite,* 2nd movement (ex. 9-4)

N.B.: "R" indicates a slight holding back (a subtle ritenuto or ritardando). "A" means to push ahead and intensify tempo (a slight accelerando).

Conductor and soloist should go over the score before rehearsal to agree upon interpretation. In performance, they should maintain rapport for the right balance of give-and-take in leadership to achieve the dramatic and expressive effects that spontaneity or, at least, the appearance of spontaneity, provides.

Conducting Activities

1. Practice between-beat anticipatory gestures for gradual tempo changes.
2. Practice the "and/prep" gesture for subito tempo changes.
3. Devise quarter-note drills, a series of quarter notes, incorporating the accelerando, ritardando, ritenuto, and subito changes of tempo. Use a mirror for initial practice. Then have your colleagues respond to your conducting the quarter notes to determine if your gradual and subito gestures are clear.
4. Practice shifting meter patterns with an accelerando from three to one and four to two.
5. Practice shifting meter patterns with a rallentando from one to three and two to four.

6. Practice following recordings of recitatives.
7. Prepare excerpts 11-1 through 11-15 in Part III, incorporating rubato and other tempo modifications as appropriate.

SELF-CHECK MASTERY TEST ━━━━━━━━━━━━━━━━━━━━

1. Lead the class in a quarter-note drill containing gradual and subito tempo changes.
2. Conduct excerpts 11-1 through 11-15, as requested by the instructor, in class using the videocassette recorder.
3. Rate your VCR performance by using the following checklist.

TEMPO VARIATIONS

Yes   No

_____ _____ Accelerando given clearly
                 Comments _____

_____ _____ Rallentando given clearly
                 Comments _____

_____ _____ Ritenuto executed
                 Comments _____

_____ _____ Between-beat anticipations used
                 Comments _____

_____ _____ Subito tempo changes prepared with "and/prep" or full-count prep
                 Comments _____

_____ _____ New tempo clear and secure
                 Comments _____

_____ _____ Meter shifts smoothly executed
                 Comments _____

_____ _____ Rubato used and executed appropriately
                 Comments _____

_____ _____ Accompaniments conducted effectively
                 Comments _____

---

learning module ***TWELVE***

Analysis and Score Preparation

OVERVIEW

This module is designed to help you study, analyze, and prepare scores for rehearsal and performance. Score study in advance of rehearsal is essential for valid interpretation, efficient rehearsing, and—especially for inexperienced conductors—developing effective manual technique. Never attempt to learn music with the performers during practice; always acquire a conception of the score through study before the rehearsal. How should the music sound? What does the composer want? How should the music move? Where is it going? How should it get there? What exactly should be accomplished in rehearsal? A conductor with integrity is above all faithful to the score. To the best of your ability, then, find out what the composer intended by analyzing the music's structure and searching for any hidden meaning within it. This process complements a conductor's musical intuition. Analysis may confirm intuition, but it may also guide you away from the possible misconceptions and faulty interpretations to which intuition might otherwise lead you. Thus, score analysis is an indispensable tool for the practicing conductor for both practical and theoretical reasons.

THE THREE BASIC STEPS OF ANALYSIS

▶ ***COMPETENCY 14***
Demonstrate ability to analyze the score for conception, interpretation, rehearsal, and performance

The primary purpose of score analysis is to achieve an aural concept—or ideal inner hearing—of the score. This inner hearing of the ideal performance guides interpretation and serves as a standard for rehearsal. The conductor compares the actual sound of the group with his or her inner sound ideal. The primary goal of the rehearsal, then, is to make the ensemble play or sing the way you imagine (know) it should play or sing by progressively eliminating errors of interpretation and technique. Furthermore, a valid inner sound image provides the only solid basis for developing your conducting skills. Conducting certainly involves more than isolated beat patterns and gestures. What you hear inside (the desired musical result) guides and shapes your manual technique to bring about the most efficient learning. Score study also helps you to anticipate problems that may arise during conducting and rehearsal, such as fermatas, cues, balance, precision, and so on. Be prepared for problems and have solutions ready.

Instruction

The following recommended procedure for score analysis consists of three interrelated steps. You should (1) acquire a conception of the music, (2) anticipate problems of conducting, and (3) anticipate problems of ensemble and rehearsal.

The Three Basic Steps

1. Acquire a conception   Your first step should be to develop an aural concept of the score through a structural and expressive analysis of the music. This analysis must include much more than the typical assignment for a class in form and analysis. For conducting purposes, score analysis should also encompass phrase movement, nuance, harmonic tension, climax, and the evolving, dynamic aspects of the musical line. It must investigate practical matters such as instrumentation, transposition, terminology, and historical context. Use the following outline as a guide for preparing scores.

1. Ascertain which instruments or vocal parts are required and study the score order.
2. Learn all transpositions and clefs involved.
3. Define all foreign and technical terms (keep a music dictionary handy). Check tempos.
4. Make a thorough formal analysis.
   a. Locate phrases and sections by indicating cadence points and cadence types. Look particularly for important divisive cadences (e.g., at double bars) that separate the major sections of the work. In choral music, read the text for meaning and phrasing. Know the meaning and the correct pronunciation of every word, especially of texts in foreign languages.
   b. Mark the score's design. What material within the score is similar? What is contrasted? In large forms indicate the use of development and variation.
   c. Note motivic manipulation and evolution. How does the composition progress and grow from within? What is the method of thematic continuation, e.g., sequence, imitation? Check melodic shapes for theme transformation.
   d. Mark the harmonic structure, i.e., the major key areas of the tonal plan. Check modulations, coloristic harmony, dissonance, harmonic tension, and climax.
   e. Determine if the composition belongs to a standard, formal type, i.e., binary, ternary, rondo, arch form, fugue, sonata-allegro, passacaglia, etc., and plan how to clarify the architecture of the work.
5. Study the dynamic plan. Check phrase climaxes and sectional climaxes. Note coloristic use of dynamics such as **sf**, **sfz**, and **fp**.
6. Consider texture and timbre for expression and balance of parts. Locate important melodies, countermelodies, and contrapuntal lines. Take note of important doublings.
7. Determine phrase types, phrase lengths, and phrase movement for rubato and accentuation.

8. Place the composition in its historical context for valid interpretation.

9. Sing through each part considering transpositions and clefs. Then arpeggiate chords from bottom to top.

10. Reduce the score at the piano. If you are not a pianist, do as much as possible; for instance, play one, two, or three lines or use your major instrument. Listen to recordings of valid interpretations to attain an overall conception.

Remember that expressive conducting depends on moving the ongoing line through to cadences as dictated by the structure or shape of the composition. Determine how tension and motion are structurally shaped in the music.

2. Anticipate problems of conducting   In the second step of score analysis, you should beat through the score to locate possible trouble spots for conducting. Because of the complexity of the full score and the need for clarity, you should mark potential conducting difficulties using a system of color coding—blue for dynamics and red for cues, for instance. Indicate such likely conducting problems as meter changes, tempo changes, cues, fermatas, dynamics, style, accents, caesuras, fractional pickup notes, subito changes of dynamics and style, asymmetrical meter groupings, phrasing, important lines, agogics, doubled parts, and definitions of musical terms. Mark entering instruments for cuing with abbreviations, such as fl., ob., cl., trp., hn., vln., and so on. Be neat and consistent. Choose problems carefully, because overmarking the score may confuse rather than clarify.

3. Anticipate problems of ensemble and rehearsal   In the third step of score analysis, you should take note of the technical and interpretive errors you expect the performers to make and of how you intend to correct them if they occur in rehearsal. Specific problems of performance include wrong notes, wrong rhythms, and also incorrect balance, style, articulation, bowing, diction, vowels, consonants, attacks, releases, intonation, tempo, phrasing, dynamics, and blend. Look especially for such frequently played errors as wrong notes at key changes, wrong rhythms at meter and tempo changes, incorrect rhythm patterns (especially ♪. ♪, ♪. ♪, and ♪. ♪♪), late attacks following rests and fractions of counts (♪ ♪♪♪ ♪♪♪♪), accidentals missed within a measure, and poor balance when all instruments have the same dynamic markings. Choirs tend to flat because ascending intervals are sung too small and descending intervals are sung too large.

You should use a full score whenever possible to rehearse an orchestra or a band efficiently. Although using a full score may be traumatic for you at first, it is essential that you have all parts in front of you to scrutinize and correct. Condensed scores or piano reductions are helpful for the analysis of structure and useful during performances to avoid excessive page turning.

Conducting Activities

1. Using the Three Basic Steps of score analysis just described as a guide, analyze the following compositions, which are complete small forms. The music for each is included in Part III: Grainger, "Ye Banks and Braes O'Bonnie Doon" (5-7); Haydn, *St. Anthony Chorale* (9-2); Holst, Second Suite, 2nd mvt. (9-3); and Vaughan Williams, *English Folk Song Suite*, 2nd mvt. (9-4).

2. Play and sing through all parts and arpeggiate the important chords of all music you conduct.

3. Analyze the scores of the Haydn *London* Symphony, 1st mvt. (12-1), the Schubert Mass in G, "Kyrie" (12-2), and the Claude Smith *Incidental*

FIGURE 12-1
Analysis of Haydn *London* Symphony (No. 104)

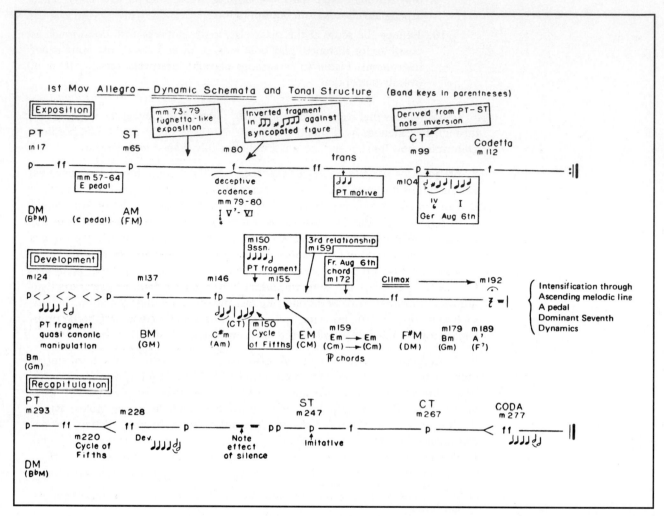

Suite (12-3), using the Three Basic Steps. Play and sing through the scores, concentrating on the transposed parts, and the parts in alto and tenor clefs. Note that some suggested bowings, fingerings, and dynamics are provided by the author in the Haydn score, and a formal analysis of the Allegro (Figure 12-1) is included in this module.

4. Beat through each score to practice specific baton techniques. Check for clarity by using a mirror.

5. After analyzing the score, listen to recordings of music you are preparing to help you establish musical conception. If possible, compare several recorded versions. Judge the most valid interpretation, using your analysis as the criterion.

SELF-CHECK MASTERY TEST ——————————————

1. Write up and submit analyses of music you are studying and conducting as requested by the instructor. Use the format of the Three Basic Steps.

2. Demonstrate knowledge of the score before and during rehearsal by attaining successful ratings on the following checklist.

SCORE PREPARATION

Before Rehearsal

Yes   No

___ ___   Sings through selected parts of the score upon receiving starting pitch
          Comments _____

___ ___   Arpeggiates any chord vocally from bottom to top
          Comments _____

___ ___   Reduces score at the piano to its essential parts
          Comments _____

During Rehearsal

___ ___   Maintains eye contact; head is out of score
          Comments _____

___ ___   Always retains place in score
          Comments _____

___ ___   Hears errors
          Comments _____

___ ___   Correctly interprets terms used in score
          Comments _____

___ ___   Gives correct transpositions
          Comments _____

The Instrumental Rehearsal

OVERVIEW

This module develops a basic rehearsal strategy and presents some specific suggestions to help you rehearse efficiently and effectively. Rehearsing is a conductor's most important job. Here, your score study and baton technique serve as the means to achieve an expressive, unified performance from the performing group. Having attained an aural concept of the score, and being in a position to listen to the whole while the musicians are intent on their parts, it is your job progressively to eliminate errors until you reach the desired interpretation.

REHEARSAL TECHNIQUE

▶ **COMPETENCY 15**
Demonstrate the ability to rehearse an instrumental group

A conductor in rehearsal is above all else a teacher. In this capacity, you use physical gestures, demonstrations, and verbal instructions to teach musicians interpretation, style, rhythmic precision, and even the notes if necessary. You identify, evaluate, and correct errors in their performance. Thus, it should not surprise you that the most effective rehearsal procedure, the one that musicians largely prefer, has the same basic format as a sound music teaching strategy: *synthesis, analysis, synthesis.* (See Figure 13-1.)

Instruction

Use the synthesis–analysis–synthesis (whole to part to whole) cycle to structure your rehearsals. In the initial **synthesis,** play through as much of a new composition as appropriate so the players can get a feeling for how it goes. At the same time, you have an opportunity to detect errors, and to locate and evaluate problems of technique, interpretation, style, balance, and so on.

FIGURE 13-1
The Basic Rehearsal Method

A	B	A Repeat as needed
SYNTHESIS	‖: ANALYSIS	SYNTHESIS :‖
Read through the music. Listen for errors.	Correct errors: Demonstrate Explain Drill Evaluate	Play through the piece again. Confirm the corrections

In the **analysis** phase of rehearsal, you should correct errors and prescribe solutions to technical and interpretative problems. The positive and efficient approach to this part-drilling phase consists of three interrelated steps. You should provide a model, provide for practice, and provide feedback. All three are essential to the process of effective rehearsal technique.

Provide a model Show the performers what is right. Demonstrate correct style, articulation, or expressive emphasis by singing it or chanting it for the group. Demonstrate correct rhythm by tapping, clapping, or counting it. Often you must explain needed corrections, that is, tell players which lines to bring out or soften for better balance, or how to finger a certain note. You may even ask a member of the group to demonstrate bowings, fingerings, tone quality, or style.

Provide for practice After the musicians have established a concept of what is right, give them a chance to practice it. Drill those sections where mistakes of technique and rhythm occurred. Repeat difficult passages several times at a slower tempo to secure physical action patterns for technical improvement and precision. Drill complex rhythm patterns on one note, or have the performers count and clap the rhythm. You can repeat chords for attacks, releases, intonation, or balance. In general, extract needed drill material from the music being rehearsed.

One director uses an effective technique with his high school band. After showing various sections what they need to accomplish and, often, how to accomplish it, he allows thirty seconds to one minute for them to work the technical problems out for themselves. Out of the bedlam comes marked improvement. The process also teaches students how to practice efficiently and productively at home.

Provide feedback Furnish players with accurate knowledge of their progress. Tell them what was right and what was wrong. If problems remain, repeat the cycle.

In the second **synthesis** phase, you should perform the music again in its entirety to confirm the results of practice and drill. If further drill is needed on errors, you repeat the process. You should assign continuing problems of technical facility to sectional rehearsals or to individual practice.

Most musicians would rather play than sit and listen to the conductor talk. Musicians certainly prefer and appreciate artistic completeness or, as it is known in gestalt psychology, "closure." Think of your own rehearsal experiences. Have you ever played for a conductor who stops every measure or two to make corrections and consequently your first complete run-through occurs at the concert? (Too much analysis.) Or have you ever worked with a conductor who continues to play through music, making few suggestions, expecting performers to correct their own mistakes? (Too much synthesis.)

In the first approach, the musicians have little opportunity to acquire a feeling for the whole, the gestalt. In the second approach, some improvement occurs in successive repetitions, but the group also practices and learns errors. The obvious answer is to make judicious use of both methods in a balance suitable for the organization and circumstance. For example, members of a professional group who know the literature and who have little rehearsal time may need no run-through. An amateur group, on the other hand, may not have the technical facility to play through some compositions without completely breaking down. Recordings can help the player achieve synthesis in this situation by serving as a model to facilitate learning. In most circumstances, however, an initial reading through the composition is possible, and preferable to tearing it apart for rehearsal drill, at the very start.

FIGURE 13-2
Rehearsing a School Group

Synthesis   Play through a complete section, or until the group breaks down. Listen for mistakes.

Analysis   Here is what a conductor can do, from the least to the most effective rehearsal technique.

Least Effective
Repeat the section without making any comments except "Let's do it again." After all, any repetition gives the players another chance to work their mistakes out for themselves. Unfortunately, it also provides an opportunity to practice and learn those mistakes.

Not Much Help
Talk about the problems in general terms or lecture the group. Admonish them to do better!
"You didn't do that very well; do it better next time!"
"Play it cleanly; tighten it up."
"Get the right notes."

Most Effective
Give specific, concise instructions: "Separate, crescendo, accent, F-sharp." But don't just tell. Show them what to do and how to do it, if necessary. Demonstrate what is correct: Count, clap, chant, sing it.

Next give players the opportunity to practice the correction. Drill them on performance problems. Then let them know how well they have done. It does little good to show or tell them what was wrong and then move on to something else. Give them feedback. Don't just move ahead or tell them it was great when it wasn't. If it wasn't correct, demonstrate and drill again.

Synthesis   Put it back together again to confirm progress. It makes us all feel good to know how we have improved.

Specific Suggestions for Rehearsing

Speak up   You must be heard, so articulate clearly and loudly enough to be understood by performers in the back rows.

Communicate   Tell the players what to correct. Give verbal directions, corrections, and demonstrations that are terse, concise, and clear, in three sentences at most. Never talk with your hands in preparatory position. Remember that a demonstration of correct performance is usually much more effective than a verbal correction.

Explain repetitions   Make stops only for specific purposes that are made clear to performers and that improve some aspect of performance, such as correcting the rhythm, improving precision, balancing parts, and so on.

Be positive   Even though you stop frequently to correct mistakes, emphasize the positive. Describe and demonstrate what is right and what players should do next time to improve performance. Do not dwell on mistakes or criticize individuals excessively.

Be demanding   Demand concentration and positive effort. Do not tolerate inattention and sloppy playing. Be the best example of what you demand.

Be punctual   Start the rehearsal on time even if only a few players are present. Soon all performers will know that rehearsals always begin promptly, and they will be ready. Similarly, end the rehearsal on time.

Waste no time   Keep the rehearsal moving. Know the score. Use clear and effective baton technique. Make the players read the stick for precision, tempo, style, dynamics, and balance, to eliminate unnecessary stops. In softer passages, call out instructions, suggestions, and corrections. When sight-reading, shout rehearsal letters to lost players. After stopping for corrections, locate the starting place by telling players to follow along with you from a rehearsal letter as you count measures out loud to the spot. They arrive when you do and save time, since they do not have to count measures again. Mark parts before rehearsal, showing bowings, measure numbers, dynamics, and so on. Post the order of music and make sure everyone has the correct part.

Use your ears   Concentrate at all times to hear mistakes. Play through the music initially to locate the most critical errors upon which to drill. You may point out potential trouble spots before you begin rehearsing, but you can never know exactly what will go wrong until you attempt a reading. (Why waste time?) Although it is difficult, if not impossible, to list an order of priority for eliminating errors, inexperienced conductors tend to emphasize the obvious in rehearsals, especially dynamics. It seems more appropriate to start by correcting fundamental problems, such as wrong notes, rhythms, style, and balance, before working on subtle dynamic shadings or fine points of intonation. Table 13-1 provides a quick reference to the types of errors a conductor may encounter in rehearsal, some possible causes of those errors, and suggestions for their correction.

Evaluate   Decide which problems need immediate attention, and which are unintentional slips that the players themselves will correct in subsequent readings. Acknowledge such obvious mistakes by looking at the offender with an expression that conveys, "Get it right next time!"

Tape the rehearsal   Use a tape recorder to assist score study at your leisure. Errors are easy to miss when you are caught up in the technical problems and excitement of conducting. Develop future rehearsal objectives from the analysis.

TABLE 13-1
Rehearsal Technique: Errors, Possible Causes, and Solutions

HEAR	POSSIBLE CAUSE	SOLUTION
Wrong notes	Out-of-key playing	Check tonality, fingerings; practice scale of key
	Key change	Point out, mark key changes; provide pencil for each folder
	Accidentals through a measure	Point out all notes affected by accidentals; mark accidentals through measure
	Written mistakes in parts	Correct mistakes in parts
	Technically difficult passages; fingering problems	Drill passages at slow tempo; require sectional and individual practice
Incorrect rhythm	Complex, hard-to-count rhythms	Demonstrate correct rhythm
	Dotted figures	Count out in unison
	Wrong accentuation or stress	Demonstrate correct accentuation (interpretation)
	Syncopations	Conduct the instruments that are *on* the beat
	Off beats for many measures	
Uneven runs	Technically difficult passages; fingering problems	Move fast notes of run evenly to longer, final note; aim for the last note
	Coordination problems	Perform slowly and evenly; work patterns accenting first note of each group, e.g., ♪♪♪♪ ♪♪♪♪
		Use alternate fingerings and positions
		Play *notes* arhythmically and *rhythms* on one note.
Asymmetrical meters played incorrectly, e.g., symmetrically	Divisions not constant	Demonstrate correct rhythm
	No aural concept of rhythm/meter	Use counting drills (see Appendix E)
		Clap divisions
Poor tone quality and control	Immature embouchures	Provide models of good tone to emulate
	Overblowing	Watch for overblowing, especially brass
	Lack of support	Check mouthpieces and reeds
	Not enough bow	Winds use support, especially *pianissimo*
		Strings bow near bridge for more volume, quality and brilliance; increase finger pressure for *piano;* use vibrato as appropriate
		Percussion use correct mallets
Tempo rushing or dragging	Technically difficult music	Check beat clarity; practice with metronome
	Conductor's beat unclear	Beat larger to stop rushing
	Not watching conductor	Beat smaller to stop dragging
		Train group to watch the stick, e.g., with quarter-note drills
Tempo vacillating, wobbly	Group doesn't hear/feel beats	Conduct the people who have beats
	Players on beats play unevenly	Give precise beat gestures; watch for excessive rebound
Wrong style	Musicians tend to play in neutral, **mf,** semilegato nonstyle	Admonish players to read around the notes; pay attention to articulation
	Musicians do not follow articulation, bowing or dynamic markings	Mark articulations and bowings in parts
		Demonstrate appropriate connection or separation
	Style not conveyed by baton	Read the stick
		Give clear style gestures
		Indicate, adjust dynamics
Bad balance and blend	Accompaniment too loud	Bring out melodic lines and important inner parts, e.g., countermelodies
	Brass and percussion too loud	Subdue other parts
	Sustained chords cover moving parts	Balance chords
		Urge players to listen, within and between sections
		Have *forte* sustained chords played *fp* or *f>* to achieve strong attack but allow moving parts to be heard

HEAR	POSSIBLE CAUSE	SOLUTION
Poor intonation	Not warmed up Not tuned properly Not attentive to pitch	Use unison warm-up routine if necessary Tune to a fixed sound source Stop often to tune notes and chords Demand good intonation at all times Urge players to listen Tune important chords, e.g., first and last, from bottom to top Check bass lines Check lines moving in 8va's; have lower 8va played strongly; have upper 8va play 8va lower to listen and hear the intervals Work out the fingerings, especially strings Play loud passages softly to listen and adjust; play short notes long and fast passages slowly
Lacking dynamic contrast	Typical inertia of musicians Inattention	Eliminate dull, dry, *mezzo-forte* by achieving extremes of ranges, especially *pianissimo* Gradually feed a crescendo, begin softly Gradually let down a diminuendo, start loudly Emphasize subito changes and **sfz, fp,** etc., for color
Phrases broken	Lack of interpretive knowledge and skill Immaturity Wind players run out of breath String players run out of bow	Move through phrase climax to cadence Maintain intensity; no breathing in the middle Release phrases together; conduct phrasing beats Stagger breathing Mark breathing/phrasing places Stagger bowings
Phrases run together	String players do not need breaks to breathe	Add breath marks (commas) to string parts
Lack of precision and ensemble	Inattention Technical difficulties	Have all musicians face the conductor; move chairs and stands Read the stick Practice precise, clean attacks and releases in style, dynamic, and tempo (see Module One and Quarter-note Drill, Appendix B) Drill technical passages slowly Stop conducting; make them listen and get it together by ear

DAILY REHEARSAL PLAN

Many authorities advocate and many band directors use a daily rehearsal plan to assure maximum efficiency for limited rehearsal time. A typical fifty-five-minute rehearsal routine follows.

Five minutes	Warm up and tune
Five minutes	Drill technique and rhythms
Twenty minutes	Rehearse and "polish" music previously presented
Twenty minutes	Sight-read and rehearse new music
Five minutes	Provide a pleasant closing by playing a well-liked, well-rehearsed, or popular composition

Outline your rehearsal on the chalkboard. List the order of music. Write out drill materials. Provide important information for students on study sheets. Have examples available for teaching musical concepts. Prepare or secure needed music and media. Finally, give careful consideration to the warm-up and drill periods.

Warm-up and tuning   Directors often use a chorale or a B-flat scale, which appears to be universal for bands, to warm up and tune. Both can be effective if students thoroughly understand their purpose. Playing a chorale or any slow passage allows students to listen for tone quality, balance, blend, and intonation as they warm up their embouchures and instruments. But this does not happen automatically. Students must be directed to listen, and be told exactly what to listen for in the music, or the warm-up and tuning period will be a waste of effort. Furthermore, tuning must continue throughout the rehearsal because young players must be reminded to listen and tune at all times. Students also tend to tune differently from the way they play. They are cold and nervous at the beginning of the period and tend to "pinch." They must be warmed up and relaxed as they play a tuning note. Taking an out-of-tune chord from the music being rehearsed during the course of the rehearsal provides an opportunity to improve intonation effectively and, in addition, learn something about chord structure.

The customary playing of scales for warm-up and tuning often results in wasted effort also. Try asking your students why they should practice scales. How many will answer in the following ways? (1) "To learn tonality (key feeling) as it relates to the music I play. This helps me to play the right notes and play them better in tune." (2) "To learn the tendencies of active and passive scale tones for more expressive playing." (3) "To gain technical facility, since most technically difficult passages in tonal music are based upon scalewise figures and runs." All those answers get to the heart of musical and technical development.

Ensemble drill   Unison drill and even drills on individual parts must be included in the regular rehearsal period if sectional rehearsals cannot be scheduled. As a rule, try to relate drills to the whole group, and always relate drills to the music being played. To illustrate: Don't study one scale or key and then practice music in another key; don't discuss one form or style and then play another; don't study a rhythm from a drill book and then play a composition that does not use that rhythm. Instead, pull drill materials from the music being performed rather than from drill books of unrelated exercises. This is a direct reversal of the usual "drill period" approach, but most effective for learning. For example, the dotted-eighth-and-sixteenth rhythm is difficult for most young groups to execute accurately. They seem to slip inevitably into a triplet feeling. Unison drill should be used every time this rhythm is found in the music being played until it is played correctly. Use the scale based upon the tonality of the composition and play the rhythm on each scale step or repeat it on the tonic.

But do not misunderstand. Technical drill books are valuable for reference, since they isolate and attack many of the most common rehearsal problems. Assign dotted rhythms and other rhythm patterns when they are not correctly played in rehearsal. Select, assign, and play scale exercises, arpeggios, and chords in the keys of the compositions being rehearsed that day. Technique books have another advantage. Parts are transposed. Therefore, students playing transposing instruments do not have to relate everything the director says from the concert pitch to their instruments. They simply read the appropriate part. Similarly, bass clef instruments do not have to adjust from written treble notation. However, the basic premise is not altered—the actual problems should derive from, and relate back to, the music being performed for learning to be most efficient and relevant. Find corresponding drills in the technique books and keep them handy for reference and use in rehearsal.

Conducting Activities

1. Observe rehearsals of selected performing groups. Use the "Rehearsal Technique" checklist in the Self-Check Mastery Test on page 76 to evaluate the rehearsals.

2. Listen continuously for mistakes as you participate in rehearsals as a performer. If you do not hear some types of errors easily (e.g., intonation or out-of-key notes), concentrate on a specific element until you improve. Can you identify mistakes the conductor misses or chooses not to deal with?

3. Rehearse music and record your rehearsals on audio tape or videotape for feedback. Study the tapes carefully and note what errors you missed. Evaluate your performance with the "Rehearsal Technique" checklist. Work to improve your voice, directions, demonstrations, error detection, and problem solution.

4. Find or develop a performing group of your own to rehearse and conduct. It is the only sure way for you to learn conducting.

SELF-CHECK MASTERY TEST ───────────────────────────────

1. Rehearse instrumental music from Part III and other scores, as requested by your instructor, in class with the videocassette recorder.
2. Rate your performance by using the following checklists.

MECHANICS OF SCORE READING

Yes   No

____ ____ Maintains eye contact; not score-bound
____ ____ Always retains place in score; not lost
____ ____ Correctly interprets terms used in score
____ ____ Gives correct transpositions

REHEARSAL TECHNIQUE

____ ____ Verbal instructions easily heard
____ ____ Verbal instructions terse and concise
____ ____ Demonstrations used to model correct performance
____ ____ Demonstrations accurate and appropriate
____ ____ Time not wasted; something accomplished every stop
____ ____ Instructions and directions sometimes given while group is playing
____ ____ Effective baton technique for ensemble problems
____ ____ Interest and concentration of group maintained
____ ____ Errors identified
____ ____ Errors corrected

PROBLEMS DETECTED AND SOLUTIONS OFFERED FOR:

Yes	No		Yes	No	
____	____	Wrong notes	____	____	Intonation
____	____	Incorrect rhythms	____	____	Technique/Facility
____	____	Style	____	____	Tempo
____	____	Balance	____	____	Blend
____	____	Precision (Attacks/Releases)	____	____	Tone
____	____	Articulation	____	____	Phrasing
____	____	Bowing	____	____	Dynamics

learning module **FOURTEEN**

The Choral Rehearsal

| **OVERVIEW**

Although general in scope, this module is designed primarily to give instrumental music specialists the basic information needed to conduct and rehearse a choral group. A noted conductor once remarked, "Conducting is conducting"; that is, there should be no difference between instrumental and choral conducting techniques. However, conductors must be prepared to use effective rehearsal techniques that are appropriate for the performance medium. Herein lies the significant difference.

REHEARSAL TECHNIQUE

▶ **COMPETENCY 16**
Demonstrate the ability to rehearse a choral group

The principal differences between instrumental and choral music are threefold: (1) Words, that is, vocalized syllables, carry the tonal line of choral music. (2) Vowel sounds, not instrumental timbre, provide choral tone color and beauty. (3) The text supplies literal, not abstract, musical meaning to the listener. Therefore, to achieve a beautiful tone and blend, the conductor in a choral rehearsal must concentrate on vowels; to achieve clarity of verbal meaning, he or she must concentrate on consonants. We see that diction must be a primary concern of every aspiring choral conductor. Since the following discussion of diction is necessarily limited, the serious student should study the excellent books on diction in singing cited in the bibliography.

Instruction

A most important goal of the choral rehearsal is to create a sustained choral tone. As a general rule for acceptable tone quality, all singers must sing on vowels, since vowels carry the tone. Amateur groups are noted for their growling *r*'s, hissing *s*'s, and affected *m*'s and *n*'s. For good tone quality and blend, then, all singers must sing on the same vowel sounds. Even native or regional pronunciations, although not acceptable for art music, will nonetheless blend chorally when all singers sing on the same vowel sounds. If, however, the choral conductor strives for standard English pronunciation that is neither provincial nor affected, and that achieves beauty and blend, all singers must sing pure or natural vowels. In English, the basic vowels are *EE, AY, AH, OH,* and *OO,* and they can be vocalized by the choir on *mee, may, mah, moh, moo.*

me   may   mah   moh   moo   me   may   mah   moh   moo   Ascend in
                                                                        half steps;
                                                                        then descend.

Another problem you will encounter when developing choral tone is the need for singers to open their mouths. Think of trying to play a brass instrument with the bell crushed shut. Not much tone can be generated. Similarly, you must get your singers to open their mouths to let the tone out. First attempts may be unsuccessful, because untrained singers do not understand how wide the mouth must extend to open up singing. Additionally, their jaws become tired. One technique is to have them place two fingers in their mouths, thumb down, to feel the extent of space needed for open vowels. The open vowels include *AH, AY, OH,* and *I (ah-ee).* Use an arpeggiated drill with breath behind it, fingers in mouth, to get the feel of open singing with support.

hah   hah   hah   hah   hah   hah   hah   hah   hah   hah   Ascend in
                                                                     half steps.

Moving from these open vowels to closed vowels *(oo, eh, ih)* is most difficult. For example, have the choir practice "Alleluia" (*Ah-leh-loo-yah,* open-closed-closed-open).

Whereas vowels achieve choral tone, consonants supply verbal meaning. Clear, precise, well-articulated consonants ensure that the verbal meaning of the text is conveyed to the listener. The choral conductor must give clean attacks for beginning consonants and must be especially concerned with phrase endings. A precise phrasing-release gesture assures precision of ensemble and clarity of meaning when the final consonant is enunciated. Closing the thumb against the fingers of the left hand is an effective technique.

Consonants are placed in two categories for singing; unvoiced consonants that have no definite pitch (as *t, p, f*), and voiced consonants that have a sustainable pitch (as *m, n, l*). Vowels and unvoiced consonants are placed on the beat where they are notated. Voiced consonants are sounded slightly before a vowel on a notated beat. Think of them as grace notes that precede the vowel on the beat. Even unvoiced consonants should be treated this way when given emphasis for dramatic effect.

This   was   my   day .

Th- i-   sw- a-   sm- ah -eed-   eh   -   ee.

Choir members often have trouble with diphthongs. Although a diphthong is a syllable that begins on one vowel sound and then moves to another, do not let choir members sing a diphthong as two vowels. Instead, treat the shorter vowel of the diphthong as a consonant. The word "day" in the preceding figure is a good example: Sustain the long "A" sound as in "eh" followed by a quick "ee." Other examples include the long "I" sung as the diphthong "ah—ee," and the long "u" sung as "ee-oo—."

As a general rule, then, for sustained, legato style with beautiful, full choral tone, sing on vowels and tack the final consonant of a syllable or word to the beginning of the next syllable or word. Have singers articulate the short vowel sound of a diphthong in this manner.

My coun - try 'tis of thee, Sweet land of lib - er - ty, Of thee I sing:
Mah -eecuh- ntree - tih-sah-vthee, Swee- tlah- ndah -vlih-beh- rtee, Uh-vthee ay -ee see -ng:

For advanced work in choral diction, study the International Phonetic Alphabet (IPA), explained thoroughly in the MENC publication *Pronunciation Guide for Choral Literature.*

Two syllables that always give trouble are the "er" as in *father* and the "i" as in *sing.* The "er" in words such as *father* and *ruler* should be sung "uh—r." Also use "uhr" when singing "ir" *(sir)*, "or" *(world)*, and "ur" *(turn).*

fath - er   sing   fah - thuh- r

The short "i" in words such as *sing, ring,* and *thing* should sound almost like a long "e," instead of the dull "ih."

FIGURE 14-1
Basic Vocal Pronunciation Chart

VOWELS
(Sing uniform, natural vowel sounds)

1. Pure vowels
   ee as in "beet"
   oo as in "boot"
   ah as in "hot"
   uh as in "hut"
   ih as in "sit"
   a as in "bat"
   eh as in "bet"
2. Diphthongs—two combined vowels
   (Sing on the first vowel and treat the second as a consonant)
   I as in "bike" *(ah +ee)*
   A as in "bake" *(eh +ee)*
   O as in "boat" *(oh +oo)*
   Others
   (ah +oo) as in "now"
   (oh +ee) as in "boy"
   (ee +oo) as in "view" (Treat first vowel as a consonant and sing on the second)

CONSONANTS
(Place before the beat)

1. Voiced
   Vocally sustainable:
   l, m, n, ng, r, th, v, w, x, y, z
   Partially sustainable:
   b, d, g, j
2. Unvoiced
   c, ch, f, h, k, p, q, s, sh, t, w

SYNTHESIS–ANALYSIS–SYNTHESIS

Use the synthesis–analysis–synthesis (whole to part to whole) cycle to rehearse new music. In the initial synthesis phase, have the choir sing through the composition to get a feel for the musical-textual meaning. Many conductors sight-sing on a neutral syllable such as "lah" after reading through the words in strict rhythm and discussing their meaning and mood. If the new music is too difficult to sight-sing, have the accompanist play the vocal parts in strict rhythm as the singers hum their parts. You may wish to use a recording as a model. Then have them sing through the music with text as well as possible. This gives you the opportunity to detect errors of rhythm, pitch, balance, style, diction, and so on.

In the analysis phase, you demonstrate and drill the choir on performance problems, starting with major flaws and continuing to fine points of interpretation and nuance. Be energetic and positive, using your singing voice and verbal imagery to get your points across. Demonstrate correct pronunciation of difficult text, indicating the exact placement of vowels and consonants in tempo and on pitch. Students repeat and mark their parts to attain precision, tone, blend, and enunciation. Drill difficult rhythms on one note, having them sing a neutral syllable such as "tah" or chant rhythm syllables. Next add the text and finally the text with music. Demonstrate and drill difficult intervals arhythmically until they are firmly in the singers' ears. Then put them back in place rhythmically. Have your singers get a physical feel for style through kinesthetic movements to "punch" a marcato section, "chop up" a staccato phrase, or "smooth out" a legato melody. If you must pound out parts to learn them, keep singers attentive by having them hum their lines while the piano drills the line of the errant section. Another time-saving device is to drill two parts simultaneously. If the choir is flatting, have them change from sitting to standing, listen to each other, think pitch, stretch ascending intervals, and shorten descending intervals. To achieve a long phrase line, stagger breathing when a breath is needed within a phrase. Have singers sneak in and out. If a soloist must breathe within a phrase, it will not break the line if the first note after the breath is sung at the same volume, intensity, and color as the note preceding the breath. In all instances, provide feedback and drill toward perfection.

Sing it through again! This subsequent synthesis phase gives you and your choir the opportunity to hear improvement and gain the satisfaction that results from a productive rehearsal.

CHORAL REHEARSAL PLAN

Planning is needed to assure maximum efficiency for limited rehearsal time. A typical fifty-five-minute daily rehearsal plan for the chorus may look something like this:

Five minutes	Warm up
Fifteen minutes	Brush up and polish music previously rehearsed
Twenty minutes	Rehearse music previously read
Ten minutes	Sight-read
Five minutes	Sing a well-liked, well-rehearsed, or popular composition

Obviously, the order of rehearsal and the relative times allotted to each activity can be shifted to accommodate the director or the circumstance, but all aspects should be covered in most rehearsals. Special consideration is given here to warm-up and rehearsal closure, since they were not mentioned earlier.

Warm-up techniques are as varied as the number of choir directors encountered. Many start with physical exercises to loosen up the body and induce proper posture and breathing. One director has students jog in place, then turn and rub each others' shoulders. A technique to promote breath support is to have singers (1) stand erect, rib cage up, shoulders relaxed, hands around waist; (2) inhale for eight counts, expand all around, without raising shoulders; and (3) exhale with a "hiss" for eight to twelve counts to feel the breath support the tone.

Vocalises are popular with most choral conductors for warm-up. Many books are available on the topic; *Voice Building for Choirs* by Ehmann and Hasseman is an excellent choice. However, the most effective approach is to develop warm-up exercises from the repertory being rehearsed that day. You can design vocalises to address the difficult intervals, tonal patterns, and rhythms found in the music. Make reference to these warm-ups during rehearsal as needed. They can also provide drill material for the specific problems found in the music.

Sing something pleasurable or exciting toward the end of the period so the rehearsal will conclude on a happy note. Singers will have a feeling of accomplishment and look forward to the next rehearsal.

Conducting Activities

1. Observe rehearsals of selected choral groups. Use the "Rehearsal Technique" checklist in the Self-Check Mastery Test on page 82 to evaluate the rehearsals.

2. Listen continuously for mistakes as you participate in rehearsals as a performer. If you do not hear some types of errors easily (e.g., intonation, flatting, blend, and diction), concentrate on a specific element until you improve. Can you identify mistakes the conductor misses or chooses not to deal with?

3. Rehearse music and record your rehearsals on audio tape or videotape for feedback. Study the tapes carefully and note what errors you missed. Evaluate your performance with the "Rehearsal Technique" checklist. Work to improve your voice, directions, demonstrations, error detection, and problem solution.

4. Find or develop a choral group of your own to rehearse and conduct, e.g., church choir or community chorus. It is the only sure way to learn choral conducting.

SELF-CHECK MASTERY TEST ────────────────────────────────

1. Rehearse the choral music from Part III and other scores, as requested by your instructor, in class with the videocassette recorder.
2. Rate your performance by using the following checklists.

MECHANICS OF SCORE READING

Yes   No

_____ _____ Maintains eye contact
_____ _____ Always retains place in score; not lost
_____ _____ Correctly interprets terms used in score

REHEARSAL TECHNIQUE

_____ _____ Verbal instructions easily heard
_____ _____ Verbal instructions terse and concise
_____ _____ Demonstrations used to model correct performance
_____ _____ Demonstrations accurate and appropriate

PROBLEMS DETECTED AND SOLUTIONS OFFERED FOR:

Yes	No		Yes	No	
___	___	Wrong notes	___	___	Diction
___	___	Incorrect rhythms	___	___	Purity/uniformity of vowels
___	___	Style	___	___	Consonants
___	___	Balance	___	___	Intonation of ensemble
___	___	Blend	___	___	Intonation of sections
___	___	Tone	___	___	Phrasing
___	___	Precision	___	___	Dynamics

PART III Musical Excerpts

LEARNING MODULE ONE

The Baton, Preparation, Downbeat, and Release

1-1 Prep-downbeat-release Study I   ADAPTED FROM BEETHOVEN

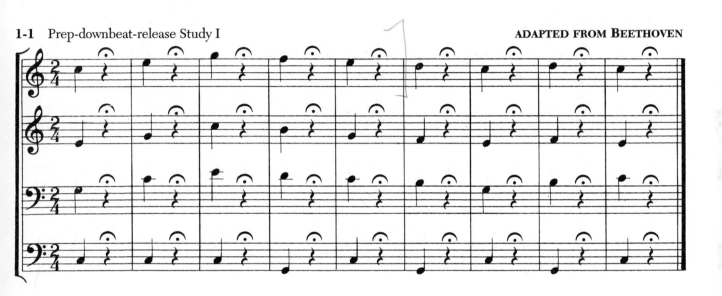

1-2 Prep-downbeat-release Study II   ADAPTED FROM DVOŘÁK

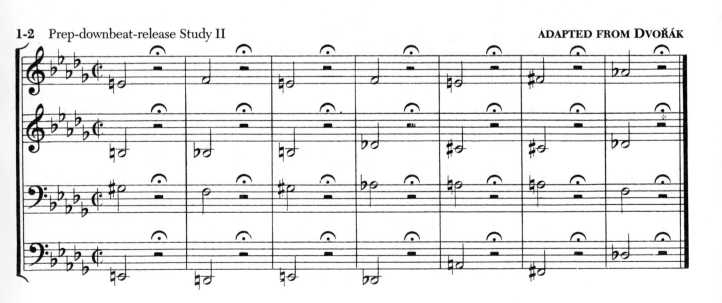

1-3 Prep-downbeat-release Study III   **ADAPTED FROM BACH**

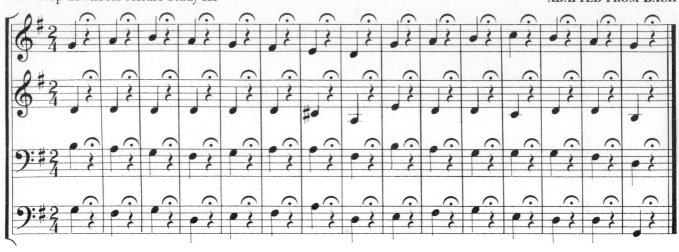

1-4 Prep-downbeat-release Study IV   **ADAPTED FROM BERLIOZ**

1-5 *Magic Flute* Overture   **W. A. MOZART**

LEARNING MODULE TWO

Beat Patterns and Preparations in Tempo, Dynamic, and Basic Style

2-1 *Xerxes,* "Largo"   G. F. HANDEL

2-2 *La Lyra* Suite, Menuet II

G. TELEMANN

2-3   Symphony no. 8 *(Unfinished),* 1st movement

F. SCHUBERT

Allegro moderato

2-4   Symphony no. 78, 1st movement   **J. HAYDN**

2-5 Symphony no. 9, 1st movement

2-6 *Enigma Variations,* Theme

2-7 *Le Prophète,* "Coronation March"

G. MEYERBEER

Tempo di marcia maestoso

2-8 Symphony no. 104, 1st movement

J. HAYDN

2-9   Symphony no. 101, 4th movement

2-10 *Russlan and Ludmilla* Overture

M. GLINKA

2-11 *The Red Mill,* "Streets of New York"

V. HERBERT

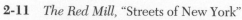

2-12 *Emperor* Waltz

Tempo di valse *(in one)*

2-13 Symphony no. 4, Scherzo

P. TCHAIKOVSKY

2-14 Symphony no. 2, 2nd movement

2-15 "America"   TRADITIONAL

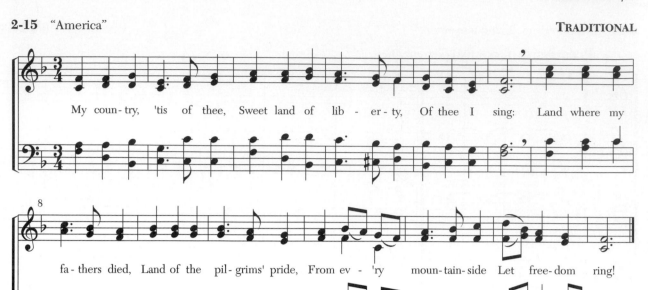

My coun-try, 'tis of thee, Sweet land of lib - er-ty, Of thee I sing: Land where my fa-thers died, Land of the pil-grims' pride, From ev - 'ry moun-tain-side Let free-dom ring!

2-16 "Chester"   W. BILLINGS

Let ty-rants shake their i - - ron rod, And Slav-'ry clank— her— gall- - - ing chains. We fear them not;— we— trust— in— God, New— Eng-land's God for ev - - - er reigns.

2-17 "O Light Divine"

A. ARCHANGELSKY

Moderato

p O Light di - vine!— The world— re - joic- es As the

mor - ning breaks— and shad - ows fly.

2-18 "Golden Slumbers"

TRADITIONAL

Slowly flowing, *in one*

p Gold - en slum - bers kiss your eyes,— Smiles— a -

wait you when you rise,— Sleep lit - tle ba by,

Sleep!— Sleep!—

do— not cry, And I will sing you lull- a- by,

Sleep!— Sleep!—

LEARNING MODULE THREE

Preparations and Releases for All Counts

3-1   Menuetto

J. HAYDN

3-2   *Aida,* "March"

G. VERDI

3-3 *A Midsummer Night's Dream, "Nocturne"* **F. MENDELSSOHN**

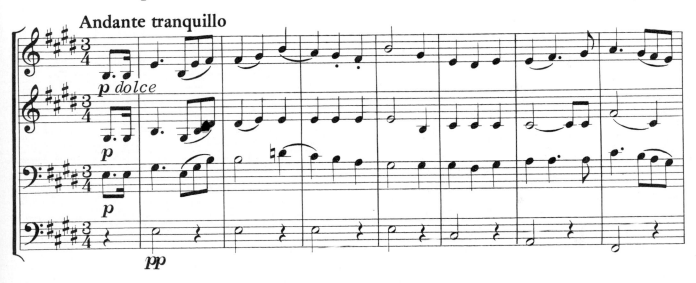

3-4 Symphony no. 94, 3rd movement

J. HAYDN

3-5 *La Lyra* Suite, "Sicilienne avec Cadenze"

G. TELEMANN

3-6   Symphony no. 5, 3rd movement, Menuetto

F. SCHUBERT

Allegro molto

3-7   Symphony no. 5, 2nd movement

F. SCHUBERT

3-8   Suite no. 3, Chaconne

J.C.F. FISCHER

3-9 Symphony no. 15, 2nd movement, Romanze

3-10   Suite no. 3, Gavotte

J.C.F. FISCHER

3-11   *La Lyra* Suite, Gigue

G. TELEMANN

3-12 "Londonderry Air"

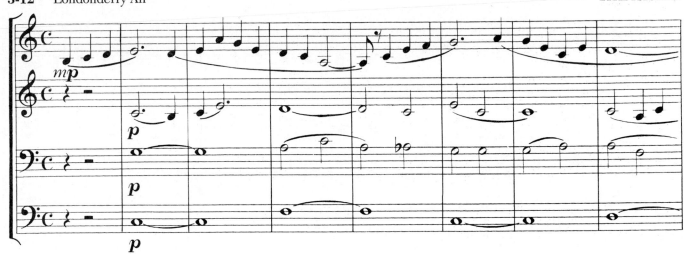

3-13 "America, the Beautiful"

S. WARD

O beau-ti-ful for spa-cious skies, For am-ber waves of grain,— For pur-ple moun-tain maj-es-ties A-bove the fruit-ed plain!— A-mer-i-ca! A-mer-i-ca! God shed His grace on thee,— And crown thy good with broth-er-hood From sea to shin-ing sea!

3-14 "When Jesus Wept"

W. BILLINGS

When Je-sus wept— the fall - - -ing tear In mer-cy flowed— be-yond all bound; When Je- - -sus groaned— a trem-bling fear seized all— the guil - - -ty world— a-round.

3-15 *Finlandia*

3-16 *Stabat Mater,* "Quando corpus" (Hear Us, Lord)

G. ROSSINI

LEARNING MODULE FOUR

Fractional Beat Preparations

4-1   Symphony no. 94, 4th movement

J. HAYDN

Allegro di molto

4-2   *Water Music* Suite, Bourrée

G. F. HANDEL

Allegro

4-3 Symphony no. 15, 4th movement

J. HAYDN

4-4 *Rosamunde* Overture

F. SCHUBERT

4-5 Symphony no. 100, 4th movement

J. HAYDN

4-6 Symphony no. 5, 4th movement

F. SCHUBERT

4-7 *Scheherezade*, Part III   N. RIMSKY-KORSAKOV

4-8   Symphony no. 6, 1st movement

P. **Tchaikovsky**

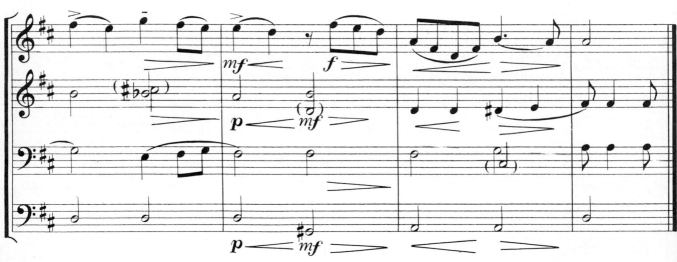

4-9 *La Lyra* Suite, Bourrée II   **G. TELEMANN**

4-10 *Symphonic Variations*   **C. FRANCK**

4-11 Symphony no. 2, 2nd movement, Scherzo   **R. SCHUMANN**

4-12 *Dido and Aeneas, "Destruction's Our Delight"*

H. PURCELL

LEARNING MODULE FIVE

Divided Meters

5-1   Concerto Grosso, 1st movement   A. VIVALDI

Adagio e spiccato

5-2   Symphony no. 7, 1st movement

Adagio

5-3   Prelude in G Minor

J. S. Bach

5-4   *Military* Symphony, 2nd movement

F. J. Gossec

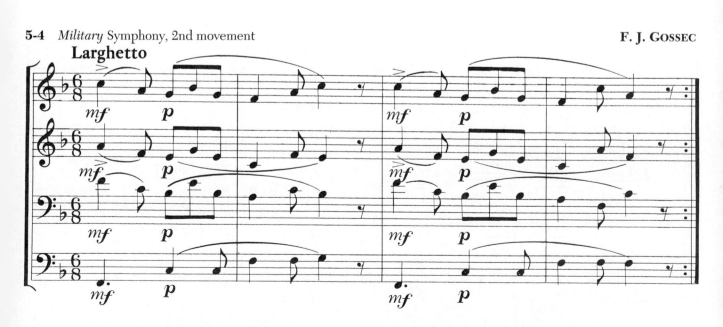

5-5 *Tristan and Isolde*, Prelude

Langsam und schmachtend

5-6 Symphony no. 1 in C Major, 2nd movement

5-7 "Ye Banks and Braes o' Bonnie Doon"

P. GRAINGER

5-8 *Prelude to "The Afternoon of a Faun"*

5-9 *Messiah,* "How Beautiful Are the Feet"   G. F. HANDEL

5-10 *The Royal Fireworks Music,* "Alla Siciliana"   G. F. HANDEL

5-11   Piccolo Concerto in C Major, 2nd movement

A. VIVALDI

5-12 *Messiah,* "Pastoral Symphony"

Larghetto e mezzo piano

5-13   "Greensleeves"   **TRADITIONAL**

LEARNING MODULE SIX

Conducting Musical Style

6-1   Symphony no. 94, 2nd movement   J. **Haydn**

6-2 Symphony no. 101, 1st movement

6-3   Prelude in E-flat Minor

D. SHOSTAKOVICH

6-4 Symphony no. 9, Finale

A. Dvořák

Original Key, Em

6-5 *Trauersinfonie* on Themes by C. M. von Weber

6-6 *Emperata Overture*   C. T. SMITH

6-7 Symphony no. 5, Finale   **D. SHOSTAKOVICH**

6-8 *L'Arlésienne* Suite no. 2, Intermezzo

6-9 "In These Delightful, Pleasant Groves"

6-10 *Dido and Aeneas,* "Great Minds Against Themselves Conspire"

H. PURCELL

most de - sire; and shun the cure they most de - sire____ they most de - sire.

cure, the cure, and shun the cure they most de - sire, the cure they most de - sire.

most de - sire; and shun the cure, the cure they most de - sire.

And shun the cure they most____ de - sire, and shun the cure they most de - sire.

LEARNING MODULE SEVEN

The Fermata

7-1   Chorale, "Wie schön leuchtet der Morgenstern"

How love-ly shines the morn-ing star! The na-tions see and hail a-far, The

How love-ly shines the morn-ing star! The na-tions see and hail a-far, The

light in Ju-dah shin-ing   Low-ly! Ho-ly! Great and glo-rious,

light in Ju-dah shin-ing   Low-ly! Ho-ly! Great and glo-rious,

Thou vic-to-rious Prince of grac-es, Fill-ing all the heav'n-ly plac-es.

Thou vic-to-rious Prince of grac-es, Fill-ing all the heav'n-ly plac-es.

7-2   Chorale, "Sei gegrüsset, Jesu gütig"   J. S. BACH

7-3 Chorale, "Ach Gott und Herr"   J. S. BACH

7-4   Symphony no. 104, 1st movement

7-5   Symphony no. 2, 1st movement

L. VAN BEETHOVEN

7-6 *Orpheus,* "Dance of the Furies"

7-7 *The Soldier's Tale, "Great Chorale"*   **I. STRAVINSKY**

7-8 *Variations on "America"* C. E. IVES

7-9 *Variations on "America"* C. E. IVES

7-10 *Variations on "America"* C. E. IVES

7-11 *Oberon* Overture

C. M. VON WEBER

7-12   Symphony no. 1, 1st movement   R. Schumann

7-13   Symphony no. 2, 1st movement   A. Borodin

7-14 Symphony no. 101, 1st movement   J. **HAYDN**

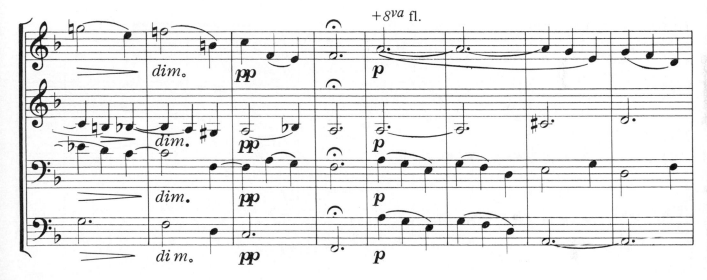

7-15 Overture for Band

Andante con moto

7-16 *Victory at Sea*

R. RODGERS

Tempo moderato

7-17 *Gigi* Selections

WORDS BY ALAN JAY LERNER AND MUSIC BY FREDERICK LOEWE

Allegretto

7-18 "The Star-Spangled Banner"

7-19 *Mlle. Modiste,* "I Want What I Want When I Want It"   V. HERBERT

7-20 *Gigi* Selections

N.B.: To execute a subito tempo change, swing up as you think "and one" in the new tempo to signal a secure preparation.

7-21 Symphony no. 5, 1st movement

L. VAN BEETHOVEN

7-22 "The Heav'ns Are Telling"

L. VAN BEETHOVEN

7-23 "Passing By"

E. PURCELL

There is a la - dye sweet and kind, Was nev - er face so pleas'd my— mind,—

I did but see her pass - ing by, And yet I love her till I die.

LEARNING MODULE EIGHT

The Cue

8-1 Fantazia no. 12

H. PURCELL

Andante

8-2   Symphony no. 40, 2nd movement

8-3 Fugue in D Minor

J. S. BACH

8-4   Fugue in C Minor   J. S. **Bach**

8-5 Chorale prelude, "O Lamm Gottes unschuldig"

J. PACHELBEL

8-6 Concerto Grosso in D Minor

A. VIVALDI

8-7 "Call to Remembrance"

8-8 *Judas Maccabaeus, "Halleluia, Amen"*   G. F. HANDEL

le - lu - ia, Hal - le - - - - lu - ia!

Hal - le - lu - ia, A - men, A - men, Hal - le - lu - ia, A - men!

Hal - le - lu - ia, A - men!

Hal - le - lu - ia, A - men, A - men, Hal - le - lu - ia, A - men!

LEARNING MODULE NINE

The Left Hand

9-1   String Quartet in D Minor, *Death and the Maiden*   F. SCHUBERT

9-2   *St. Anthony* Divertimento, Chorale   **FORMERLY ATTRIBUTED TO J. HAYDN**

9-3   Second Suite in F, 2nd movement, "Song Without Words"   **G. Holst**

9-4 *English Folksong Suite*, 2nd movement

R. VAUGHAN WILLIAMS

Andantino

9-5 Symphony no. 4, 2nd movement

Andante con moto

9-6 *Rienzi* Overture

Molto sostenuto e maestoso (♩ = 66)

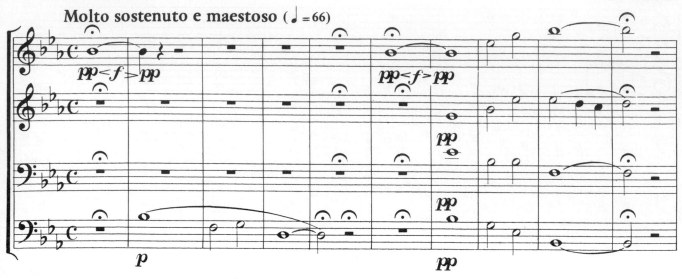

9-7 *Enigma Variations, "Nimrod"*

E. ELGAR

9-8 *Psyché et Éros*

Allegretto modéré

9-9 *Egmont* Overture, 2nd theme

L. van Beethoven

9-10 Piano Concerto no. 2, 1st movement

Allegro con brio

9-11 *Orlando Palandrino* Overture   J. Haydn

9-12 *The Impresario* Overture

9-13 *Firebird* Ballet, "Infernal Dance"   **I. STRAVINSKY**

9-14 *Symphonie fantastique,* "March to the Scaffold"

9-15 "God So Loved the World"

J. STAINER

9-16 "O Bone Jesu"

9-17 *Dido and Aeneas,* "In Our Deep Vaulted Cell" *(in the manner of an echo)*   H. PURCELL

9-18 "Bless the Lord, O My Soul"

M. IPPOLITOF-IVANOF

LEARNING MODULE TEN

Asymmetrical and Changing Meters

10-1 *Tales of Hoffman,* Entr'acte

J. OFFENBACH

10-2 *Lincolnshire Posy,* 2nd movement, "Harkstow Grange"

P. GRAINGER

10-3 Symphony no. 6, 2nd movement

Allegro con grazia (♩ = 144)

10-4 *El Amor Brujo, "Pantomime"*

M. DE FALLA

10-5   *Firebird* Ballet, Finale°   **I. STRAVINSKY**

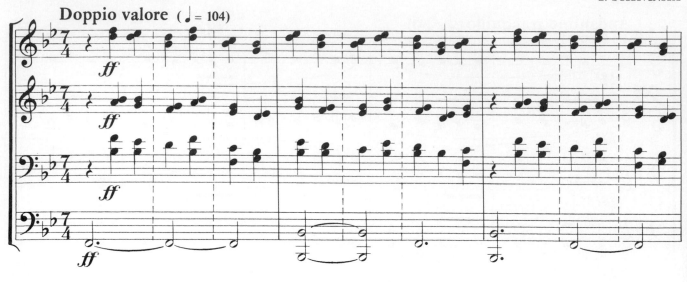

°May be performed in original key of B-natural.

10-6   *Fanfare for Brass*   **J. HARTWAY**

10-7 Symphony no. 12, 1st movement

10-8   Five-eight Study (2 + 3). Uneven Meter in Two.
Adapted from Scherzo, Symphony no. 3

A. BORODIN

10-9   Five-eight Study (3 + 2). Uneven Meter in Two

ADAPTED FROM BLAZHEVICH

10-10 Seven-eight Study (2 + 2 + 3). Uneven Meter in Three

10-11 Seven-eight Study (3 + 2 + 2). Uneven Meter in Three

ADAPTED FROM BLAZHEVICH

10-12 Suite in F for Band, 3rd movement

F. M. Breydert

10-13 *Lincolnshire Posy,* 5th movement, "Lord Melbourne"   P. GRAINGER

10-14 *Carmina Burana, "Uf dem Anger"*

C. ORFF

10-15   *The Soldier's Tale, "Royal March"*

10-16   *Lincolnshire Posy*, 3rd movement, "Poaching Song"   P. GRAINGER

10-17 *The Rite of Spring* Ballet, "Glorification of the Chosen One"

10-18 *Three of e.e.'s*   J. HARTWAY

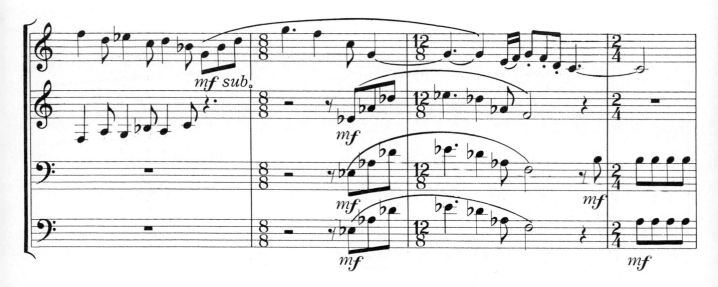

10-19 "Ave Maria"

A - ve Ma - ri - a, gra - ti - a ple - na,

Do - mi - nus te - cum, A - ve Ma - ri - a.

10-20 "Cry Out with Joy"   CHRISTOPHER WALKER

From "Cry Out with Joy" by Christopher Walker. Copyright © 1975 by Oxford University Press, Inc. Used by permission.

10-21 "O Clap Your Hands"

M. Thomas Cousins

10-22 "Sing We Merrily"

GORDON KING

LEARNING MODULE ELEVEN

Tempo Changes and Accompanying

11-1 Symphony no. 9, 4th movement

A. DVOŘÁK

11-2 Symphony no. 2, 1st movement   R. SCHUMANN

11-3 *Die Fledermaus* Overture

11-4 *Egmont* Overture, 1st theme

11-5 *Egmont* Overture, Coda

Allegro con brio

[Accel. 4 to 2]

11-6 *Victory at Sea*

Tango

11-7 *Magic Flute* Overture

11-8 *Cosi Fan Tutte* Overture

Presto (in 2)

11-9 *Nabucco* Overture

11-10   Symphony no. 1, 4th movement   **L. van Beethoven**

11-11 *Mlle. Modiste* Selections

V. HERBERT

11-12 *Messiah*, no. 14, "There Were Shepherds Abiding in the Field"

Recitative

There were shep-herds a - bid-ing in the field, keep-ing watch o-ver their flocks by night.

11-13 *Messiah,* no. 19, "Then Shall the Eyes of the Blind"   G. F. HANDEL

°The orchestral cadence traditionally performed *after* the solo cadence.

11-14 *Christ on the Mount of Olives,* no. 3, Recitativo

L. VAN BEETHOVEN

death to make a-tone-ment, so long the race of man is cast a - way, de-priv'd of an- y part of life e- ter - nal.

11-15 *Le Coq d'Or,* "Hymn to the Sun"

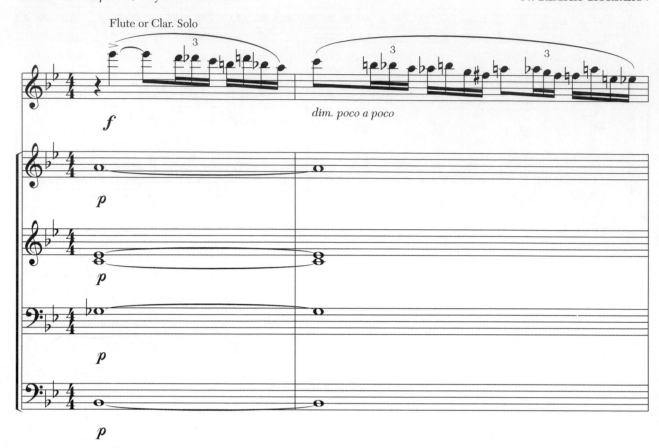

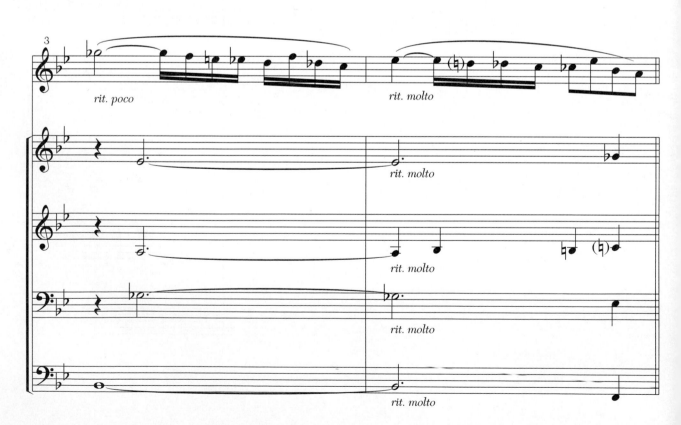

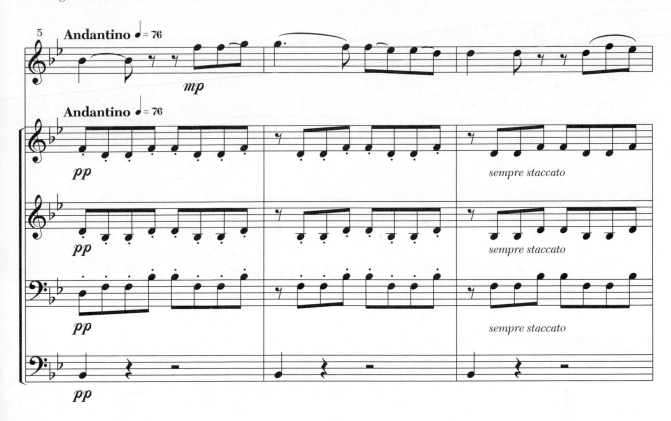

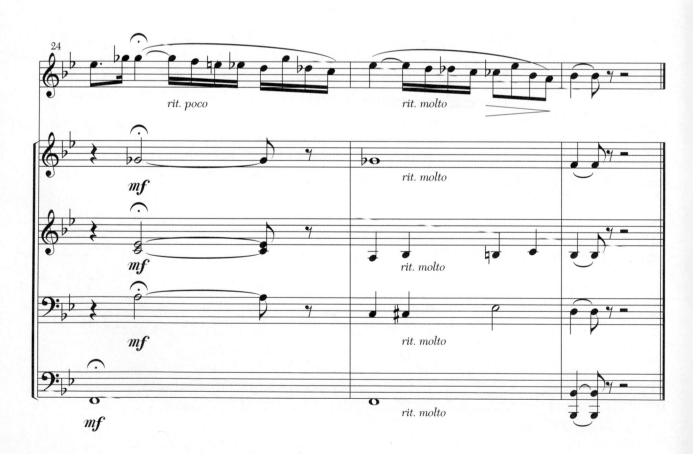

11-15 *Le Coq d'Or*, "Hymn to the Sun," flute solo

11-15   *Le Coq d'Or,* "Hymn to the Sun, clarinet solo   N. RIMSKY-KORSAKOV

LEARNING MODULE TWELVE

Analysis and Score Preparation

12-1 Symphony no. 104 (*London*), 1st movement, complete   J. **HAYDN**

260

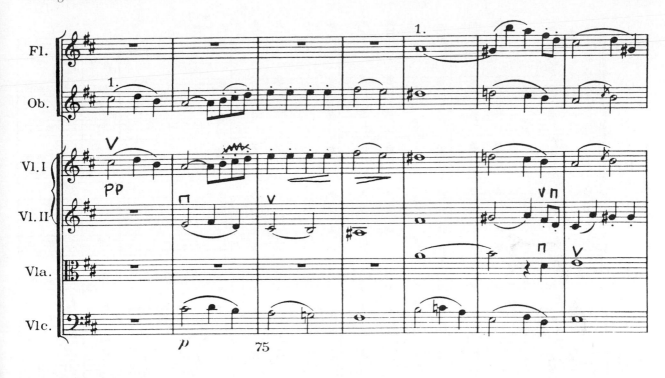

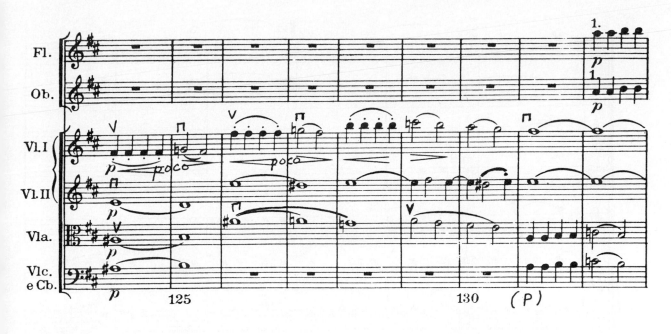

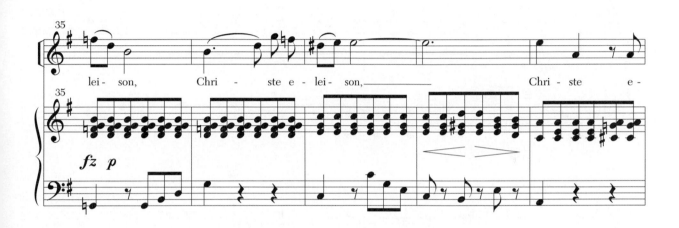

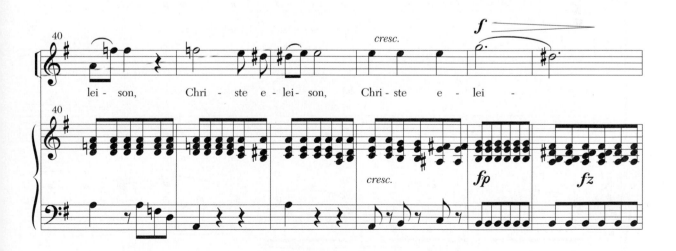

12-3 *Incidental Suite,* Tarantella

C. SMITH

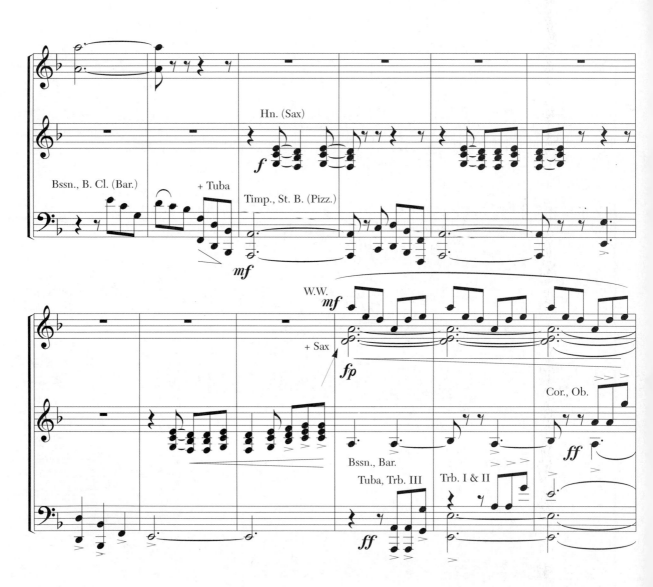

Rondo

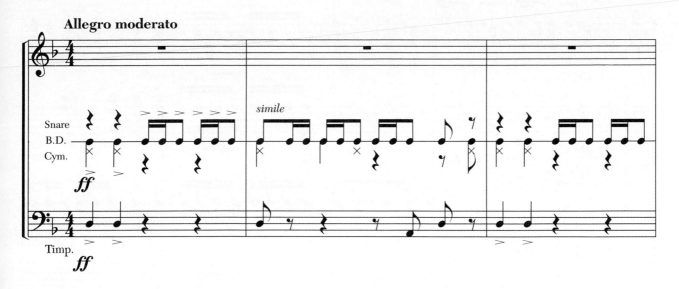

°Play A to B one time **ff** on D.S.

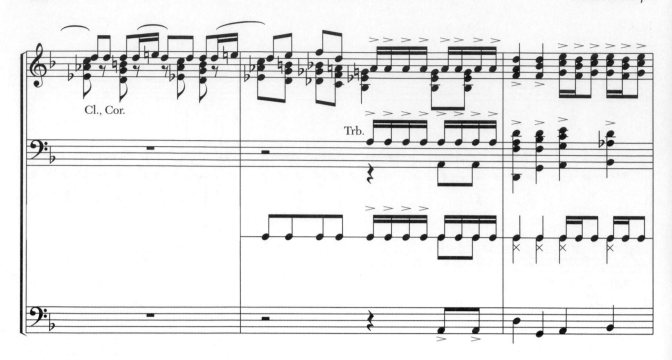

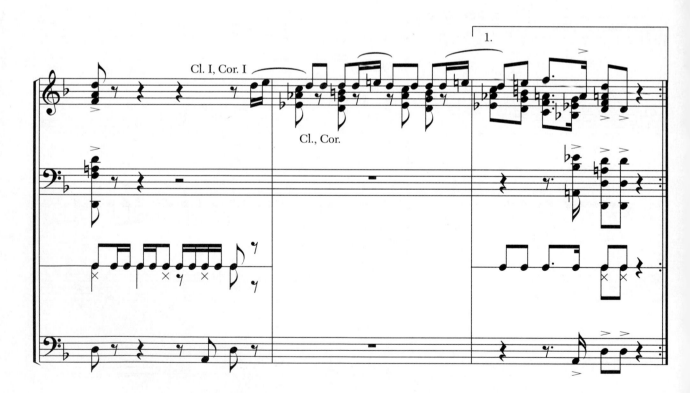

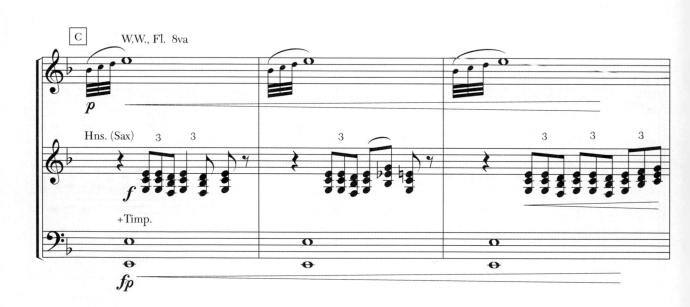

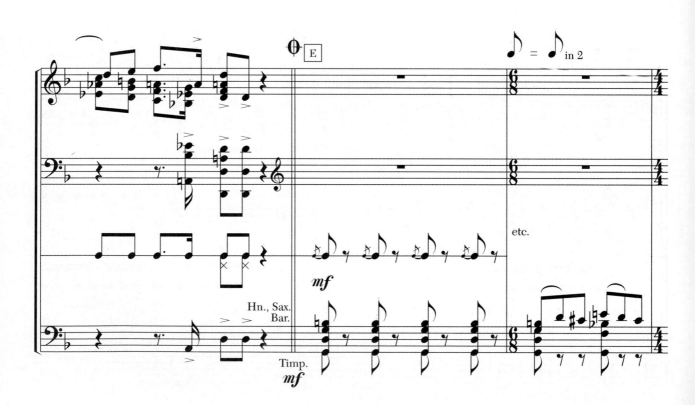

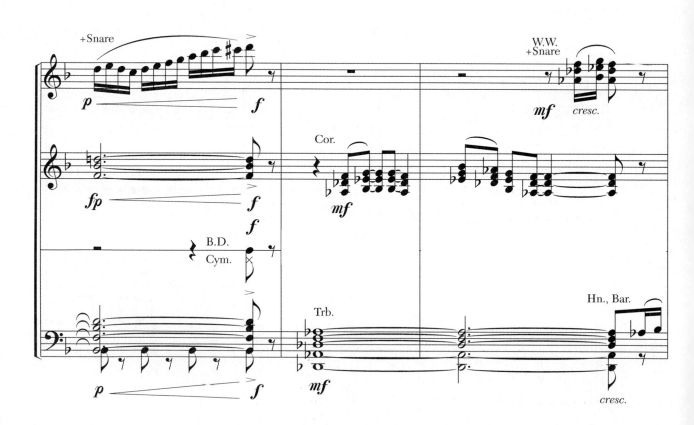

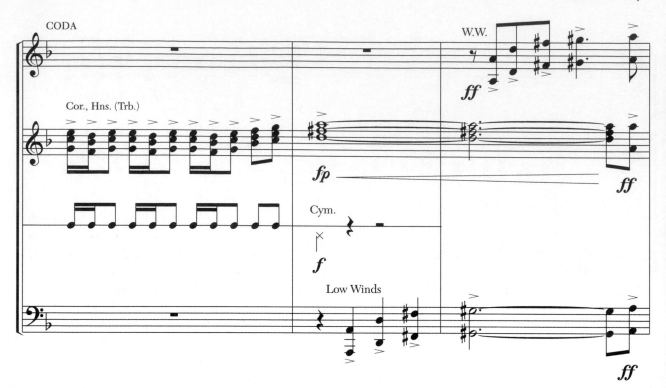

APPENDIX A
Competencies for the Beginning Conducting Class

The following list of competencies was arrived at by an analysis of the essential skills a beginning conductor should develop to lead and rehearse a performing organization. These competencies form the basis of the learning modules in this workbook. The Quarter-Note Drill in Appendix B provides an effective exercise for practicing many of the competencies. The Conducting Competence Rating Scale, also in Appendix B, evaluates student performance of the competencies.

Conducting Techniques

The beginning conducting student will:

1 Demonstrate appropriate baton grip.

2.1 Demonstrate the preparatory position for starting on the count of one in all meters.

2.2 Demonstrate the preparatory position for starting on counts other than one.

3.1 Demonstrate the preparatory beat for the count of one, i.e., for the downbeat in all meters.

3.2 Demonstrate the preparatory beat for the count of one that indicates appropriate tempo, dynamic level, and style of music being performed.

3.3 Demonstrate the preparatory beat for counts other than one.

3.4 Demonstrate the preparatory beat that indicates appropriate tempo, dynamic level, and style for fractional pickup notes and between-beat starts.

4 Demonstrate proper wrist action to define the exact point of beat.

5.1 Demonstrate the basic release gesture.

5.2 Demonstrate the release on all counts of all meters.

6 Demonstrate the standard beat patterns, maintaining a steady tempo.

7 Demonstrate beat divisions in simple and compound meters.

8 Demonstrate styles of beating, including the legato, staccato, marcato, tenuto, and neutral (nonexpressive) beat styles.

9.1 Demonstrate the fermata, with a release and caesura of appropriate length, and a subsequent preparatory beat.

9.2 Demonstrate the fermata, with the release gesture used as a preparatory beat.

9.3 Demonstrate the fermata, without release but with a preparatory gesture to signal resumption.

10 Demonstrate cuing gestures with the left hand, baton, and nod of head, with eye contact and preparation for each.

11 Demonstrate independent and effective use of the left hand to signal dynamics, subito changes, accents, phrasing, and balance.

12 Demonstrate changing meters and asymmetrical patterns in slow and fast tempos.

13 Demonstrate gradual and subito changes in tempo and the ability to accompany.

Score Preparation and Rehearsal Technique

14 Demonstrate ability to analyze the score for conception, interpretation, rehearsal, and performance.

15 Demonstrate the ability to rehearse an instrumental group.

16 Demonstrate the ability to rehearse a choral group.

APPENDIX B
Student Evaluation

CONDUCTING COMPETENCE RATING SCALE*

Conductor _____ Rater _____

Use letters to rate each major heading. Write comments to clarify and justify your marks.

A—a superior performance; few errors or omissions
B—an above average performance; some minor errors and omissions
C—an average performance; several errors and omissions
D—a below average performance; many errors and omissions
E—an unacceptable performance; not prepared; not effective

Read the explanatory material before attempting to rate.

Rating

_____ 1. Preparatory Position
Comments _____

_____ 2. Preparatory Beats, Anticipatory Gestures, and Attacks
Comments _____

_____ 3. Point of Beat and Standard Beat Patterns
Comments _____

_____ 4. Use of Right Hand (releases, fermatas, cues)
Comments _____

_____ 5. Use of Left Hand (dynamics, accents, cues, balance, phrasing)
Comments _____

_____ 6. Style, Interpretation, Phrasing
Comments _____

_____ 7. Knowledge of Score and Eye Contact
Comments _____

_____ 8. Rehearsal Technique (detection and correction of errors)
Comments _____

_____ 9. Overall Effectiveness
Comments _____

*You may make photcopies of this form to allow for successive ratings, or the rating of one performance by several colleagues.

How to Use the Conducting Competence Rating Scale

The Conducting Competence Rating Scale was developed to rate the overall skill attainment of the beginning conducting student. It provides for comprehensive assessment of the conducting competencies listed in Appendix A. The student should use the rating scale toward the end of the module sequence for self-evaluation of composite conducting and rehearsal techniques. The instructor can use it as part of the final examination.

The rating scale contains nine rather broad areas for you to mark. Carefully read the explanation of each component before you begin rating. Try to keep as many specific items in mind as possible. Comment on their presence or absence, and mark how well they are achieved by the conductor.

1. Preparatory position   Posture erect, poised. Position of attention easily visible and commanding. Baton held correctly; in position for prep to follow. Visual check made to ensure readiness of group. Attention of performers secured and maintained; doesn't talk with hands in preparatory position or take too much time.

2. Preparatory beats, anticipatory gestures, and attacks   Preparatory beat initiated on plane with a wrist flick, with inevitable-looking follow-through (no hesitation and no extra motions). Breathes in with upswing. Prep beat indicates tempo, dynamic level, and style. Visual contact maintained through downbeat. Attack precise. Fractional beats prepared (two ways).

Preparatory or anticipatory gestures used for all tempo changes, for resumptions after holds, for subito changes of dynamics and style, and for cues.

3. Point of beat and standard beat patterns   Ictus (point of beat) clear; beats defined by wrist action. Downbeat straight down; rebounds not too high. Beats bounce off plane of beating. Standard meter patterns correct or appropriate for music. Patterns well-defined, well-proportioned, and positioned in front of body. Pattern size fits music. Asymmetrical meters retain even divisions.

4. Use of right hand   Releases clear, concise, prepared, and in the dynamic and style of music. Fermatas executed with moving baton and for an appropriate duration; resumption prepared (three types demonstrated). Baton advanced toward players for cue.

5. Use of left hand   Left hand independent of right. Gives crescendo, diminuendo, subito changes of dynamics and style, accents, cues, balance, support for holds and final tones, nuance, and phrasing.

6. Style, interpretation, phrasing   Conducts general styles of staccato, legato, marcato, tenuto, neutral. Appropriate tempo and tempo modifications. Phrases indicated by movement and release. Gives climaxes, accentuation, dynamics, nuance.

7. Knowledge of score and eye contact   Prepared, not score-bound. Maintains visual contact for cues, preps, and so on. Always retains place in score. Instructions and demonstrations indicate knowledge of score. Sings parts. Correctly interprets terms in score. Gives transpositions.

8. Rehearsal technique (detection and correction of errors)   Verbal instructions easily heard; terse and concise. Time not wasted. Demonstrations used effectively; clap, tap rhythm, and so on. Drills on needed parts. (List errors conductor identified and corrected.)

9. Overall effectiveness   Gets results; improves performance. Has control; leads, does not follow. Has enthusiasm; maintains interest of performers.

THE QUARTER-NOTE DRILL

The quarter-note drill is an effective device for practicing and demonstrating mastery of conducting gestures that express fermatas, dynamics, and styles. The purpose of such an exercise is to elicit the desired responses from performers by means of gesture alone. Only the student conductor and the instructor have copies of the music. The drill can be performed on a predetermined pitch, on pitches from a pentatonic or whole-tone scale, or as an aleatoric work. Performance parameters require musicians to play only quarter notes and to respond as well as they can to the conductor's expressive gestures.

Specifications for a Quarter-Note Drill

1. Write out 24 to 48 quarter notes.
2. Mark them off into measures, using at least three different meter signatures.
3. The following items must be included at least once:
   a. One *each* of the *three types* of holds
   b. Crescendo
   c. Diminuendo
   d. Subito *f* to *p*
   e. Subito *p* to *f*
   f. Accented notes
   g. Styles of marcato, staccato, and legato
4. Make *two* copies.

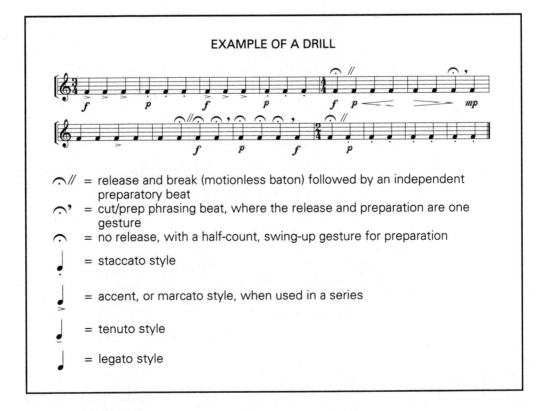

APPENDIX C
Chart of Transpositions and Clefs

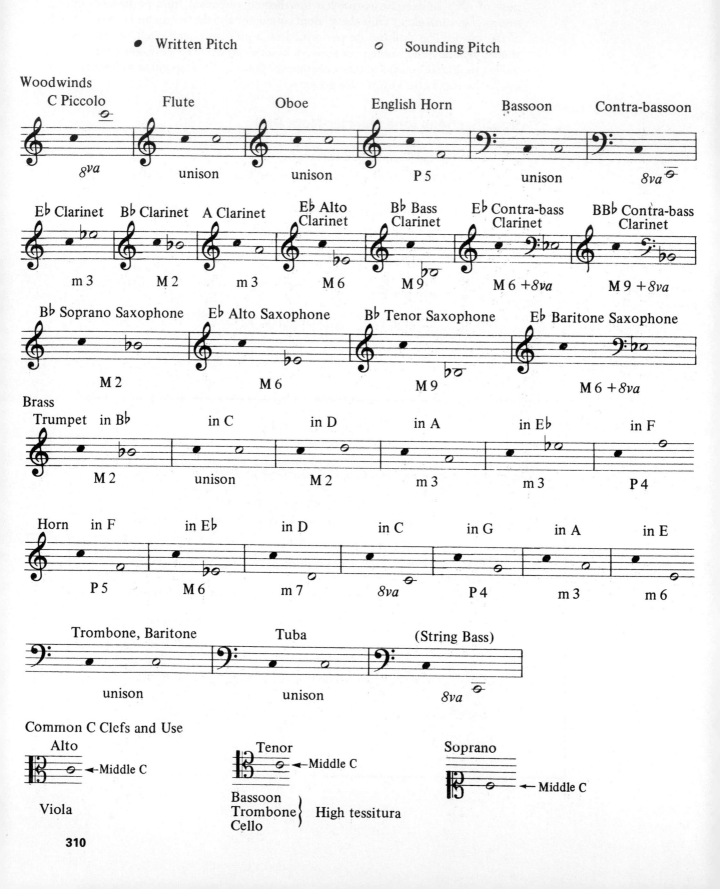

● Written Pitch   ○ Sounding Pitch

Woodwinds
C Piccolo — *8va* · Flute — unison · Oboe — unison · English Horn — P 5 · Bassoon — unison · Contra-bassoon — *8va*

E♭ Clarinet — m 3 · B♭ Clarinet — M 2 · A Clarinet — m 3 · E♭ Alto Clarinet — M 6 · B♭ Bass Clarinet — M 9 · E♭ Contra-bass Clarinet — M 6 +*8va* · BB♭ Contra-bass Clarinet — M 9 +*8va*

B♭ Soprano Saxophone — M 2 · E♭ Alto Saxophone — M 6 · B♭ Tenor Saxophone — M 9 · E♭ Baritone Saxophone — M 6 +*8va*

Brass
Trumpet in B♭ — M 2 · in C — unison · in D — M 2 · in A — m 3 · in E♭ — m 3 · in F — P 4

Horn in F — P 5 · in E♭ — M 6 · in D — m 7 · in C — *8va* · in G — P 4 · in A — m 3 · in E — m 6

Trombone, Baritone — unison · Tuba — unison · (String Bass) — *8va*

Common C Clefs and Use
Alto ←Middle C
Viola

Tenor ←Middle C
Bassoon, Trombone, Cello } High tessitura

Soprano ←Middle C

310

APPENDIX D
Full Score Instrumentation and Foreign Equivalents

ENGLISH	ITALIAN	GERMAN	FRENCH
Piccolo	Flauto piccolo	Klein Flöte	Petite Flûte
Flute	Flauto	Flöte	Flûte
Oboe	Oboe	Hoboe	Hautbois
English Horn	Corno Inglese	Englisch Horn	Cor Anglais
Clarinet	Clarinetto	Klarinette	Clarinette
Bass Clarinet	Clarinetto basso	Bassklarinette	Clarinette basse
Bassoon	Fagotto	Fagott	Basson
Contrabassoon	Contrafagotta	Kontrafagott	Contre-basson
Saxophone	Sassofono	Saxophon	Saxophone
French Horn	Corno	Horn	Cor
Trumpet	Tromba	Trumpete	Trompette
Cornet	Cornetto	Cornett	Cornet-a-pistons
Trombone	Trombone	Posaune	Trombone
Tuba	Tuba di basso	Basstuba	Tuba Basse
Kettledrums	Timpani	Pauken	Timbales
Snare Drum	Tamburo	Kleine Trommel	Caisse claire
Bass Drum	Gran cassa	Grosse Trommel	Grosse caisse
Cymbals	Piatti	Becken	Cymbales
Gong	Tam-tam	Tam-tam	Tam-tam
Triangle	Triangolo	Triangel	Triangel
Xylophone	Silifono	Sylophon	Sylophone
Tambourine	Tamburino	Tamburin	Tambour de Basque
Castanets	Castagnett	Kastagnetten	Castagnettes
Chimes	Campani	Glocken	Cloches
Bells	Campanelli	Glockenspiel	Carillon
Harp	Arpa	Harfe	Harpe
Violin	Violino	Violine	Violon
Viola	Viola	Bratsche	Alto
Cello	Violoncello	Violoncell	Violoncelle
Double Bass	Contrabasso	Kontrabass	Contrebasse

APPENDIX E
Counting Drills for Uneven Meters

This appendix provides counting drills for selected excerpts, in asymmetrical and mixed meters, to assist your score preparation and conducting practice. When studying asymmetrical meters, you must determine at the outset the proper grouping of beats and beat divisions by secondary accents. For example, the five-eight movement from Tchaikovsky's Sixth Symphony (excerpt 10-3) is always conducted 2 + 3 to match the melodic grouping and quasi-waltz character, although the accompaniment erroneously suggests a 3 + 2 grouping. In most compositions, however, the accompaniment and bass line offer the best clue to the correct grouping.

The Rite of Spring Ballet (ex. 10-17)

The Soldier's Tale, "Royal March" (ex. 10-15)

alto line

tenor line

Carmina Burana, "Uf dem Anger" (ex. 10-14)

Suite in F for Band, 3rd movement (ex. 10-12)

Three of e.e.'s (ex. 10-18)

APPENDIX F
Music Style Chart

PERIOD NAME	MUSICAL FORMS	MATERIALS
Baroque **1600–1750**	Concerto grosso Fugue Chaconne, passacaglia Suite Opera Oratorio	Melodic sequence, spun out Long, irregular phrases Infrequent cadencing Fast harmonic rhythm Imitation Monothematic Figured bass (continuo) Tonal polyphony
Classical **1750–1820**	Sonata-allegro Rondo Song form Symphony Concerto Theme & variations	Short, symmetrical phrase Action-reaction phrase Frequent cadencing Slow harmonic rhythm Simple harmony Homophonic texture
Romantic **1820–1900**	Symphonic poem Music drama Symphonic variations Concerto Symphony Overture	Lyricism Chromatic themes Long sequences Chromatic harmony Harmonic color Instrumental color
Twentieth Century **1900–**	Neo-classic Serial organization Computer music Free form Aleatoric Jazz Multidivision of ensemble	Melodic fragmentation Dissonance saturation Polytonality Atonality Linear Polymeter Changing meters Multi-forces, textures, and densities of sound

PERFORMANCE PRACTICE	COMPOSERS
Emphasize the beat	Bach
Separate longer notes, and run faster notes together (do not separate or lighten the fast notes)	Handel
Use terraced dynamics (not long cresc. or dim.)	Vivaldi
Emphasize melody/bass polarity	Corelli
Balance polyphonic lines	Frescobaldi
Play ornamentation on the beat	Purcell
Start trill on trill note	
Emphasize the measure	Mozart
Use light, precise, restrained articulation	Haydn
Lighten staccatos, separate; underplay brass	Gluck
Use refined dynamics (*sf* equals emphasis)	Gossec
Play feminine cadences as stress to release	Beethoven
Project melodic lines for clarity	
Thin parts in band transcriptions; check original perc.	
Emphasize phrasing, shadings, and climaxes	Wagner
Use rubato molto and vibrato	Brahms
Use heavy and intense tone and articulation	Tchaikovsky
Use wide range of dynamics	Liszt
Gradually "feed" long crescendos	Berlioz
Emphasize color effects: harmony, dissonance, orchestration, *sfz, forte-piano,* etc.	Mendelssohn
	Franck
	Schubert
Emphasize rhythm	Stravinsky
Play divisions evenly in asymmetrical rhythms and meters	Bartók
Carefully execute all markings of dynamics, tempo, articulation, and style	Schoenberg
Balance dissonances and extended chord structures	Hindemith
Balance lines (linear concept)	Shostakovich
Interpret neo-classic and neo-romantic compositions by referring to the related styles above	Milhaud
	Wm. Schuman
	Persichetti

Selected References

The following books are recommended supplementary reading for students working through the learning modules.

BAMBERGER, CARL, ed., *The Conductor's Art*. New York: McGraw-Hill Book Company, 1965.

This valuable anthology contains classic essays by twenty-four renowned conductors, past and present, on technical and historical aspects of conducting.

DECKER, HAROLD A., and COLLEEN J. KIRK, *Choral Conducting: Focus on Communication*. Englewood Cliffs, N.J.: Prentice Hall, 1988.

Read the sections on score preparation, repertory, vocal production, and diction for the choral singer.

EARHART, WILL, *The Eloquent Baton*. New York: M. Witmark & Sons, 1931.

Read Chapters Six, "Phrasing"; Seven, "The Phrasing-Beat"; and Eight, "Other Properties of the Beat."

EHMANN, WILHELM, and FRANKE HASSEMANN, *Voice Building for Choirs*. Chapel Hill, N.C.: Hinshaw Music, Inc., 1982.

This book is an excellent resource for selecting warm-ups to develop choral tone, and for preparing warm-up exercises related to the repertory being rehearsed.

GREEN, ELIZABETH A. H., *The Modern Conductor* (5th ed.). Englewood Cliffs, N.J.: Prentice Hall, 1993.

This book should be in every student's personal library. Refer to it often regarding manual technique, expressive gestures, cuing, transpositions, score study, and bowings.

GREEN, ELIZABETH A. H., and NICOLAI MALKO, *The Conductor's Score*. Englewood Cliffs, N.J.: Prentice Hall, 1985.

See especially Chapters Three, "Studying the Score"; Four, "Marking the Score"; Six, "Rehearsing the Score"; and Eight, "The Contemporary Score."

GROSBAYNE, BENJAMIN, *Techniques of Modern Orchestral Conducting* (2nd ed.). Cambridge, Mass.: Harvard University Press, 1973.

Read Chapters Twenty-one, "Studying and Analyzing an Orchestral Score"; Twenty-three, "Preparing for the Rehearsal"; and Twenty-four, "The Rehearsal."

HALL, WILLIAM D., ed., *Latin Pronunciation According to Roman Usage*. Tustin, Calif.: National Music Publishers, 1971.

HEFFERAN, CHARLES W., *Choral Music: Technique and Artistry*. Englewood Cliffs, N.J.: Prentice Hall, 1982.

Read this invaluable text for a concise but comprehensive coverage of choral artistry, vocal technique, diction, and choral technique.

KAPLAN, ABRAHAM, *Choral Conducting*. New York: W. W. Norton & Co., Inc., 1985.

LABUTA, JOSEPH A., *Teaching Musicianship in the High School Band*. West Nyack, N.Y.: Parker Publishing Company, 1972.

Read Chapters Seven, "How to Enhance Musicianship by Teaching the General Styles of Music," and Eleven, "How to Teach Musicianship Through Interpreting the Score."

LEINSDORF, ERICH, *The Composer's Advocate: A Radical Orthodoxy for Musicians*. New Haven: Yale University Press, 1981.

Read this book for insights into score preparation, composers and their music, traditions, performance practices, tempos, and the conductor's role.

MAY, WILLIAM V., and CRAIG TOLIN, *Pronunciation Guide for Choral Literature*. Reston, Va.: Music Educators National Conference, 1987.

MARSHALL, MADELINE, *The Singers Manual of English Diction*. New York: Schirmer Books, 1953.

McELHERAN, BROCK, *Conducting Technique* (2nd ed.). New York: Oxford University Press, 1989.

This small book is packed with many excellent ideas. Read it all.

MELCHER, ROBERT A., and WILLARD F. WARCH, *Music for Score Reading*. Englewood Cliffs, N.J.: Prentice Hall, 1971.

Use this book to study score reading, transpositions, and clefs.

PRAUSNITZ, FREDERIK, *Score and Podium: A Complete Guide to Conducting*. New York: W. W. Norton & Co., Inc., 1983.

This text presents the two basic aspects of conducting—score knowledge and baton technique—in a parallel, logical sequence. His analysis of beat gestures is extensive and insightful.

RUDOLF, MAX, *The Grammar of Conducting* (3rd ed.). New York: G. Schirmer, 1994.

Read the chapters on styles of beating patterns, holds, sudden changes of dynamics and articulation, phrasing, score study, and rehearsal techniques.

WALTER, BRUNO, *Of Music and Music-Making*, trans. Paul Hamburger. New York: W. W. Norton & Co., Inc., 1961.

Read Chapters Two, "Of Music-Making," and Three, "The Conductor."

Index of Musical Excerpts

Arcadelt, Jacques
  "Ave Maria" (10-19)
Archangelsky, Alexander
  "O Light Divine" (2-17)

Bach, Johann Sebastian
  Chorale, "Ach Gott und Herr" (7-3)
           "Sei gegrüsset, Jesu gütig" (7-2)
           "Wie schön leuchtet der Morgenstern" (7-1)
  Fugue in C Minor (8-4)
  Fugue in D Minor (8-3)
  Prelude in G Minor (5-3)
Beethoven, Ludwig van
  Egmont Overture, 1st Theme (11-4)
                2nd theme (9-9)
                Coda (11-5)
  "The Heav'ns Are Telling" (7-22)
  Mount of Olives, no. 3, Recitativo (11-14)
  Piano Concerto no. 2, 1st mvt. (9-10)
  Symphony no. 1, 4th mvt. (11-10)
  Symphony no. 2, 1st mvt. (7-5)
  Symphony no. 5, 1st mvt. (7-21)
Berlioz, Hector
  Symphonie fantastique, "March to the Scaffold" (9-14)
Billings, William
  "Chester" (2-16)
  "When Jesus Wept" (3-14)
Bizet, Georges
  L'Arlésienne Suite no. 2, Intermezzo (6-8)
  Symphony no. 1, 2nd mvt. (5-6)
Borodin, Alexander
  Symphony no. 2, 1st mvt. (7-13)
                2nd mvt. (2-14)

Breydert, Frederick M.
   Suite in F for Band, 3rd mvt. (10-12)

Conducting Drills
   Five-Eight Study, Uneven Meter in Two (10-8, 10-9)
   Preparation-Downbeat-Release Study (1-1, 1-2, 1-3, 1-4)
   Seven-Eight Study, Uneven Meter in Three (10-10, 10-11)
Cousins, M. Thomas
   "O Clap Your Hands" (10-21)

Debussy, Claude
   Prelude to "The Afternoon of a Faun" (5-8)
Dvořák, Antonin
   Symphony no. 9, Finale (6-4, 11-1)

Elgar, Edward
   Enigma Variations, Theme (2-6)
                        "Nimrod," Variation IX (9-7)

Falla, Manuel de
   El Amor Brujo, "Pantomime" (10-4)
Farrant, Richard
   "Call to Remembrance" (8-7)
Fischer, Johann Caspar Ferdinand
   Suite no. 3, Chaconne (3-8)
               Gavotte (3-10)
Franck, César
   Psyché et Éros (9-8)
   Symphonic Variations (4-10)

Glinka, Mikhail
   Russlan and Ludmilla Overture (2-10)
Gluck, Christoph
   Orpheus, "Dance of the Furies" (7-6)
Gossec, François
   Military Symphony, 2nd mvt. (5-4)
Grainger, Percy
   Lincolnshire Posy, 2nd mvt., "Harkstow Grange" (10-2)
                    5th mvt., "Lord Melbourne" (10-13)
                    3rd mvt., "Poaching Song" (10-16)
   "Ye Banks and Braes o' Bonnie Doon" (5-7)

Handel, George Frideric
   Judas Maccabaeus, "Halleluia, Amen" (8-8)
   Messiah, "How Beautiful Are the Feet" (5-9)
            "Pastoral Symphony" (5-12)
            "Then Shall the Eyes of the Blind" (11-13)
            "There Were Shepherds Abiding in the Field" (11-12)
   The Royal Fireworks Music, "Alla Siciliana" (5-10)
   Water Music Suite, Bourrée (4-2)
   Xerxes, "Largo" (2-1)
Hartway, James
   Fanfare for Brass (10-6)
   Three of e.e.'s (10-18)

Haydn, Josef
  Menuetto (3-1)
  Orlando Paladino Overture (9-11)
  St. Anthony Divertimento, Chorale [formerly attributed to Haydn] (9-2)
  Symphony no. 7, 1st mvt. (5-2)
  Symphony no. 15, 2nd mvt. (3-9)
                  4th mvt. (4-3)
  Symphony no. 78, 1st mvt. (2-4)
  Symphony no. 94, 2nd mvt. (6-1)
                  3rd mvt. (3-4)
                  4th mvt. (4-1)
  Symphony no. 100, 4th mvt. (4-5)
  Symphony no. 101, 1st mvt., Presto (6-2)
                   1st mvt., Adagio (7-14)
                   4th mvt. (2-9)
  Symphony no. 104, 1st mvt., Allegro (2-8)
                   1st mvt., Adagio (7-4)
                   1st mvt. (complete) (12-1)
Herbert, Victor
  Mlle. Modiste, "I Want What I Want When I Want It" (7-19)
                  Selections (11-11)
  Red Mill, "Streets of New York" (2-11)
Holst, Gustav
  Second Suite in F, 2nd mvt. (9-3)

Ippolitof-Ivanof, Mikhail
  "Bless the Lord, O My Soul" (9-18)
Ives, Charles
  Variations on "America" (7-8, 7-9, 7-10)

Key, Francis Scott (words to traditional melody)
  "The Star-Spangled Banner" (7-18)
King, Gordon
  "Sing We Merrily" (10-22)

Loewe, Frederick
  Gigi Selections (7-17, 7-20)

Mendelssohn, Felix
  A Midsummer Night's Dream, Nocturne (3-3)
  Overture for Band (7-15)
  Symphony no. 4, 2nd mvt. (9-5)
Meyerbeer, Giacomo
  Le Prophète, "Coronation March" (2-7)
Mozart, Wolfgang Amadeus
  Così fan Tutte Overture (11-8)
  The Impresario Overture (9-12)
  Magic Flute Overture (1-5, 11-7)
  Symphony no. 40, 2nd mvt. (8-2)

Offenbach, Jacques
  Tales of Hoffman, Entr'acte (10-1)
Orff, Carl
  Carmina Burana, "Uf dem Anger" (10-14)

Pachelbel, Johann
  "O Lamm Gottes unschuldig" (8-5)

Palestrina, Giovanni Pierluigi da
  "O Bone Jesu" (9-16)
Purcell, Edward C.
  "Passing By" (7-23)
Purcell, Henry
  Dido and Aeneas, "Destruction's Our Delight" (4-12)
                "Great Minds Against Themselves Conspire" (6-10)
                "In Our Deep Vaulted Cell" (9-17)
  Fantazia no. 12 (8-1)
  "In These Delightful Pleasant Groves" (6-9)

Rimsky-Korsakov, Nikolai
  Le Coq d'Or, "Hymn to the Sun" (11-15)
  Scheherezade, Part III (4-7)
Rodgers, Richard
  Victory at Sea (7-16, 11-6)
Rossini, Gioacchino
  Stabat Mater, "Quando Corpus" (Hear Us, Lord) (3-16)

Schubert, Franz
  Mass in G Major, "Kyrie" (12-2)
  Rosamunde Overture (4-4)
  String Quartet in D Minor, *Death and the Maiden* (9-1)
  Symphony no. 5, 2nd mvt. (3-7)
                3rd mvt. (3-6)
                4th mvt. (4-6)
  Symphony no. 8 *(Unfinished),* 1st mvt. (2-3)
  Symphony no. 9, 1st mvt. (2-5)
Schumann, Robert
  Symphony no. 1, 1st mvt. (7-12)
  Symphony no. 2, 1st mvt. (11-2)
                2nd mvt. (4-11)
Shostakovitch, Dmitri
  Prelude in E-flat Minor (6-3)
  Symphony no. 5, Finale (6-7)
  Symphony no. 12, 1st mvt. (10-7)
Sibelius, Jean
  Finlandia (3-15)
Smith, Claude T.
  Emperata Overture (6-6)
  Incidental Suite, "Tarantella" (12-3)
                "Rondo" (12-3)
Stainer, John
  "God So Loved the World" (9-15)
Strauss, Johann
  Emperor Waltz (2-12)
  Die Fledermaus Overture (11-3)
Stravinsky, Igor
  Firebird Ballet, "Danse Infernale" (9-13)
                Finale (10-5)
  The Rite of Spring Ballet, "Glorification of the Chosen One" (10-17)
  The Soldier's Tale, "Great Chorale" (7-7)
                "Royal March" (10-15)

Tchaikovsky, Peter
  Symphony no. 4, 3rd mvt. (2-13)
  Symphony no. 6, 1st mvt. (4-8)
                2nd mvt. (10-3)

Telemann, Georg
 La Lyra Suite, Bourrée II (4-9)
     Gigue (3-11)
     Menuet II (2-2)
     "Sicilienne avec cadenze" (3-5)
Traditional
 "America" (2-15)
 "Golden Slumbers" (2-18)
 "Greensleeves" (5-13)
 "Londonderry Air" (3-12)

Vaughn Williams, Ralph
 English Folksong Suite, 2nd mvt. (9-4)
Verdi, Giuseppe
 Aida, "March" (3-2)
 Nabucco Overture (11-9)
Vivaldi, Antonio
 Concerto Grosso in G Minor, 1st mvt. (5-1)
 Concerto Grosso in D Minor, Adagio and Allegro (8-6)
 Piccolo Concerto in C Major, 2nd mvt. (5-11)

Wagner, Richard
 Rienzi Overture (9-6)
 Trauersinfonie (6-5)
 Tristan and Isolde, Prelude (5-5)
Walker, Christopher
 "Cry Out with Joy" (10-20)
Ward, Samuel
 "America, the Beautiful" (3-13)
Weber, Carl Maria von
 Oberon Overture (7-11)